DOVER · THRIFT · EDITIONS

Selected Essays

MICHEL DE MONTAIGNE

DOVER PUBLICATIONS, INC.
Mineola, New York

DOVER THRIFT EDITIONS

GENERAL EDITOR: STANLEY APPELBAUM
EDITOR OF THIS VOLUME: PHILIP SMITH

Copyright

Published in Canada by General Publishing Company, Ltd., 30 Lesmill Road, Don Mills, Toronto, Ontario.

Published in the United Kingdom by Constable and Company, Ltd., 3 The Lanchesters, 162–164 Fulham Palace Road, London W6 9ER.

Bibliographical Note

This Dover edition, first published in 1996, is a new selection of essays reprinted from *Essays of Montaigne*, translated by Charles Cotton (edited by William Carew Hazlitt), published by Reeves and Turner, London, 1877. A new introductory Note and some footnotes have been specially prepared for the present edition.

Library of Congress Cataloging-in-Publication Data

Montaigne, Michel de, 1533–1592.
  [Essais. English. Selections]
  Selected essays / Michel de Montaigne.
      p.   cm. — (Dover thrift editions)
  ISBN 0-486-29109-X (pbk.)
  I. Title.   II. Series.
PQ1642.E6   1996
844'.3 — dc20   95–49132
                                                                              CIP

Manufactured in the United States of America
Dover Publications, Inc., 31 East 2nd Street, Mineola, N.Y. 11501

Note

THE *Essays* of French nobleman Michel de Montaigne (1533–1592) represent the beginning of the essay as a species of writing. Montaigne called his reflective prose works "essais" (in the sense of "attempts") to accentuate their tentative and personal qualities: they make no claims to objectivity or conclusiveness, choosing rather to focus on their author's awareness of and reactions to stated topics. In form they are leisurely and meandering, conforming only to the contours of memory and fancy, seldom submitting to the disciplines of rhetoric. It is a testament to the quality and depth of Montaigne's thought that the results of this permissive method so rarely stray into self-indulgence: instead, they illumine the workings and particularities of an individual mind as few writings have before or since, while displaying an ironical blend of skepticism and common sense that has come to symbolize the spirit of the Renaissance.

This volume contains eight essays selected from the 107 written and revised by Montaigne between 1571 and 1588. The translation used is the influential one of English poet Charles Cotton (1630–1687), as edited by William Carew Hazlitt in 1877. Bracketed editorial matter has been added by the editors of the present collection.

Contents

---

* [The numbering of the essays herein follows modern practice and differs from that of source text in some instances.]

That It Is Folly to Measure Truth and Error by Our Own Capacity

'TIS NOT, perhaps, without reason, that we attribute facility of belief and easiness of persuasion, to simplicity and ignorance; for I fancy I have heard belief compared to the impression of a seal upon the soul, which by how much softer and of less resistance it is, is the more easy to be impressed upon. "Ut necesse est, lancem in libra, ponderibus impositis, deprimi, sic animum perspicuis cedere."[1] By how much the soul is more empty and without counterpoise, with so much greater facility it yields under the weight of the first persuasion. And this is the reason that children, the common people, women, and sick folks, are most apt to be led by the ears. But then, on the other hand, 'tis a foolish presumption to slight and condemn all things for false that do not appear to us probable; which is the ordinary vice of such as fancy themselves wiser than their neighbours. I was myself once one of those; and if I heard talk of dead folks walking, of prophecies, enchantments, witchcrafts, or any other story I had no mind to believe,

> "Somnia, terrores magicos, miracula, sagas,
> Nocturnos lemures, portentaque Thessala,"[2]

I presently pitied the poor people that were abused by these follies. Whereas I now find, that I myself was to be pitied as much, at least, as they; not that experience has taught me anything to alter my former opinions, though my curiosity has endeavoured that way; but reason has instructed me, that thus resolutely to condemn anything for false and impossible, is arrogantly and impiously to circumscribe and limit the will of God, and the power of our mother nature, within the bounds of my own capacity, than which no folly can be greater. If we give the

---

[1] "As the scale of the balance must give way to the weight that presses it down, so the mind must of necessity yield to demonstration." — Cicero, Acad., ii. 12.

[2] "Dreams, magic terrors, marvels, sorceries, hobgoblins, and Thessalian prodigies." — Horace, Ep., ii. 3, 208.

names of monster and miracle to everything our reason cannot comprehend, how many are continually presented before our eyes? Let us but
consider through what clouds, and as it were groping in the dark, our
teachers lead us to the knowledge of most of the things about us;
assuredly we shall find that it is rather custom than knowledge that takes
away their strangeness —

> "Jam nemo, fessus saturusque videndi,
> Suspicere in cœli dignatur lucida templa;"[3]

and that if those things were now newly presented to us, we should think
them as incredible, if not more, than any others.

> "Si nunc primum mortalibus adsint
> Ex improviso, si sint objecta repente,
> Nil magis his rebus poterat mirabile dici,
> Aut minus ante quod auderent fore credere gentes."[4]

He that had never seen a river, imagined the first he met with to be
the sea; and the greatest things that have fallen within our knowledge,
we conclude the extremes that nature makes of the kind.

> "Scilicet et fluvius qui non est maximus, ei'st
> Qui non ante aliquem majorem vidit; et ingens
> Arbor, homoque videtur, et omnia de genere omni
> Maxima quæ vidit quisque, hæc ingentia fingit."[5]

"Consuetudine oculorum assuescunt animi, neque admirantur, neque
requirunt rationes earum rerum, quas semper vident."[6] The novelty,
rather than the greatness of things, tempts us to inquire into their causes.
We are to judge with more reverence, and with greater acknowledgment
of our own ignorance and infirmity, of the infinite power of nature. How
many unlikely things are there testified by people worthy of faith, which,
if we cannot persuade ourselves absolutely to believe, we ought at least
to leave them in suspense; for, to condemn them as impossible, is by a

---

[3] "Weary of the sight, now no one deigns to look up to heaven's lucid temples." — Lucretius,
ii. 1037. The text has *satiate videndi*.

[4] ["If they should now suddenly be present to mortals for the first time, if they should
unexpectedly be cast in his way, it would not be possible for anything to be called more
remarkable than these things, or less imaginable to peoples of the past." — Lucretius, ii. 1032.]

[5] "A little river seems to him who has never seen a larger river, a mighty stream; and so with
other things — a tree, a man — anything appears greatest of the kind that never knew a
greater." — Idem, vi. 674.

[6] "Things grow familiar to men's minds by being often seen; so that they neither admire, nor
are inquisitive about, things they daily see." — Cicero, De Natura Deor., lib. ii. 38.

temerarious presumption to pretend to know the utmost bounds of possibility. Did we rightly understand the difference betwixt the impossible and the unusual, and betwixt that which is contrary to the order and course of nature, and contrary to the common opinion of men, in not believing rashly, and on the other hand, in not being too incredulous, we should observe the rule of *Ne quid nimis*, enjoined by Chilo.[7]

When we find in Froissart, that the Count de Foix[8] knew in Bearn the defeat of John, King of Castile, at Juberoth the next day after it happened, and the means by which he tells us he came to do so, we may be allowed to be a little merry at it, as also at what our annals report, that Pope Honorius, the same day that King Philip Augustus died at Mantes, performed his public obsequies at Rome, and commanded the like throughout Italy, the testimony of these authors not being, perhaps, of authority enough to restrain us. But what if Plutarch, besides several examples that he produces out of antiquity, tells us, he knows of certain knowledge, that in the time of Domitian, the news of the battle lost by Antony in Germany, was published at Rome, many days' journey from thence, and dispersed throughout the whole world, the same day it was fought; and if Cæsar was of opinion, that it has often happened, that the report has preceded the incident,[9] shall we not say, that these simple people have suffered themselves to be deceived with the vulgar, for not having been so clear-sighted as we? Is there anything more delicate, more clear, more sprightly, than Pliny's judgment, when he is pleased to set it to work? Anything more remote from vanity? Setting aside his learning, of which I make less account, in which of these excellences do any of us excel him? And yet there is scarce a young schoolboy that does not convict him of untruth, and that pretends not to instruct him in the progress of the works of nature.

When we read in Bouchet the miracles of St. Hilary's relics, away with them: his authority is not sufficient to deprive us of the liberty of contradicting him; but generally and offhand to condemn all suchlike stories, seems to me a singular impudence. That great St. Augustin[10] testifies to have seen a blind child recover sight upon the relics of St. Gervaise and St. Protasius at Milan; a woman at Carthage cured of a cancer, by the sign of the cross made upon her by a woman newly baptized; Hesperius, a familiar friend of his, to have driven away the

---

[7] Μηδέν ἄγαν. ["Nothing to excess."] Aristotle in his Rhetoric, lib. xi. cap. 12, and Pliny (Nat. Hist., lib. vii. cap. 32) ascribe this maxim to Chilo, as does Diogenes Laertius in the "Life of Thales," lib. i. sec. 41, but he afterwards ascribes it to Solon, in his "Life of Solon," lib. i. sec. 63. It has been also attributed to others.

[8] In 1385.

[9] Civil Wars, iii. 36.

[10] De Civ. Dei, xxii. 8.

spirits that haunted his house, with a little earth of the sepulchre of our Lord; which earth, being also transported thence into the church, a paralytic to have there been suddenly cured by it; a woman in a procession, having touched St. Stephen's shrine with a nosegay, and rubbing her eyes with it, to have recovered her sight, lost many years before; with several other miracles of which he professes himself to have been an eyewitness: of what shall we accuse him and the two holy bishops, Aurelius and Maximinus, both of whom he attests to the truth of these things? Shall it be of ignorance, simplicity, and facility; or of malice and imposture? Is any man now living so impudent as to think himself comparable to them in virtue, piety, learning, judgment, or any kind of perfection? "Qui ut rationem nullam afferrent, ipsa auctoritate me frangerent."[11] 'Tis a presumption of great danger and consequence, besides the absurd temerity it draws after it, to contemn what we do not comprehend. For after, according to your fine understanding, you have established the limits of truth and error, and that, afterwards, there appears a necessity upon you of believing stranger things than those you have contradicted, you are already obliged to quit your limits. Now, that which seems to me so much to disorder our consciences in the commotions we are now in concerning religion, is the Catholics dispensing so much with their belief. They fancy they appear moderate, and wise, when they grant to their opponents some of the articles in question; but, besides that they do not discern what advantage it is to those with whom we contend, to begin to give ground and to retire, and how much this animates our enemy to follow his blow: these articles which they select as things indifferent, are sometimes of very great importance. We are either wholly and absolutely to submit ourselves to the authority of our ecclesiastical polity, or totally throw off all obedience to it: 'tis not for us to determine what and how much obedience we owe to it. And this I can say, as having myself made trial of it, that having formerly taken the liberty of my own swing and fancy, and omitted or neglected certain rules of the discipline of our Church, which seemed to me vain and strange: coming afterwards to discourse of it with learned men, I have found those same things to be built upon very good and solid ground and strong foundation; and that nothing but stupidity and ignorance makes us receive them with less reverence than the rest. Why do we not consider what contradictions we find in our own judgments; how many things were yesterday articles of our faith, that to-day appear no other than fables? Glory and curiosity are the scourges of the soul; the last prompts us to thrust our noses into everything, the other forbids us to leave anything doubtful and undecided.

---

[11] "Who, though they should give me no reason for what they affirm, convince me with their sole authority." — Cicero, Tusc. Quæs., i. 21.

Of Friendship

HAVING CONSIDERED THE proceedings of a painter that serves me, I had a mind to imitate his way. He chooses the fairest place and middle of any wall, or panel, wherein to draw a picture, which he finishes with his utmost care and art, and the vacuity about it he fills with grotesques, which are odd fantastic figures without any grace but what they derive from their variety, and the extravagance of their shapes. And in truth, what are these things I scribble, other than grotesques and monstrous bodies, made of various parts, without any certain figure, or any other than accidental order, coherence, or proportion?

"Desinit in piscem mulier formosa superne."[1]

In this second part I go hand in hand with my painter; but fall very short of him in the first and the better, my power of handling not being such, that I dare to offer at a rich piece, finely polished, and set off according to art. I have therefore thought fit to borrow one of Estienne de la Boetie, and such a one as shall honour and adorn all the rest of my work — namely, a discourse that he called Voluntary Servitude; but, since, those who did not know him have properly enough called it "Le contre Un."[2] He wrote in his youth[3] by way of essay, in honour of liberty against tyrants; and it has since run through the hands of men of great learning and judgment, not without singular and merited commendation; for it is finely written, and as full as anything can possibly be. And yet one may confidently say it is far short of what he was able to do; and if in that more mature age, wherein I had the happiness to know him, he had taken a design like this of mine, to commit his thoughts to writing, we should have seen a great many rare things, and such as would have gone very near to have rivalled the best writings of antiquity: for in

---

[1] "A fair woman in her upper form terminates in a fish's tail." — Horace, De Arte Poetica, v. 4.

[2] ["Against One."]

[3] "Not being as yet eighteen years old." — Edition of 1588.

natural parts especially, I know no man comparable to him. But he has left nothing behind him, save this treatise only (and that too by chance, for I believe he never saw it after it first went out of his hands), and some observations upon that edict of January,[4] made famous by our civil wars, which also shall elsewhere, peradventure, find a place. These were all I could recover of his remains, I to whom, with so affectionate a remembrance, upon his death-bed, he by his last will bequeathed his library and papers, the little book of his works only excepted, which I committed to the press.[5] And this particular obligation I have to this treatise of his, that it was the occasion of my first coming acquainted with him; for it was showed to me long before I had the good fortune to know him; and gave me the first knowledge of his name, proving the first cause and foundation of a friendship, which we afterwards improved and maintained, so long as God was pleased to continue us together, so perfect, inviolate, and entire, that certainly the like is hardly to be found in story, and amongst the men of this age, there is no sign nor trace of any such thing in use; so much concurrence is required to the building of such a one, that 'tis much, if fortune bring it but once to pass in three ages.

There is nothing to which nature seems so much to have inclined us, as to society; and Aristotle says,[6] that the good legislators had more respect to friendship, than to justice. Now the most supreme point of its perfection is this: for, generally, all those that pleasure, profit, public or private interest create and nourish, are so much the less beautiful and generous, and so much the less friendships, by how much they mix another cause, and design, and fruit in friendship, than itself. Neither do the four ancient kinds, natural, social, hospitable, venerian, either separately or jointly, make up a true and perfect friendship.

That of children to parents is rather respect: friendship is nourished by communication, which cannot by reason of the great disparity, be betwixt these, but would rather perhaps offend the duties of nature; for neither are all the secret thoughts of fathers fit to be communicated to children, lest it beget an indecent familiarity betwixt them; nor can the advices and reproofs, which is one of the principal offices of friendship, be properly performed by the son to the father. There are some countries where 'twas the custom for children to kill their fathers; and others, where the fathers killed their children, to avoid their being an impediment one to another in life; and naturally the expectations of the one depend upon the ruin of the other. There have been great philosophers who have made nothing of this tie of nature, as Aristippus for one, who[7]

---

[4] 1562, which granted to the Huguenots the public exercise of their religion.

[5] Paris, 1571, *chez* Frederic Morel.

[6] Moral. ad Nicomac., viii.

[7] Diogenes Laertius, ii. 31.

being pressed home about the affection he owed to his children, as being come out of him, presently fell to spit, saying, that this also came out of him, and that we also breed worms and lice; and that other, that Plutarch endeavoured to reconcile to his brother;[8] "I make never the more account of him," said he, "for coming out of the same hole." This name of brother does indeed carry with it a fine and delectable sound, and for that reason, he and I called one another brothers: but the complication of interests, the division of estates, and that the wealth of the one should be the poverty of the other, strangely relax and weaken the fraternal tie: brothers pursuing their fortune and advancement by the same path, 'tis hardly possible, but they must of necessity often jostle and hinder one another. Besides, why is it necessary that the correspondence of manners, parts, and inclinations, which begets the true and perfect friendships, should always meet in these relations? The father and the son may be of quite contrary humours, and so of brothers: he is my son, he is my brother; but he is passionate, ill-natured, or a fool. And moreover, by how much these are friendships that the law and natural obligation impose upon us, so much less is there of our own choice and voluntary freedom; whereas that voluntary liberty of ours has no production more promptly and properly its own than affection and friendship. Not that I have not in my own person experimented all that can possibly be expected of that kind, having had the best and most indulgent father, even to his extreme old age, that ever was, and who was himself descended from a family for many generations famous and exemplary for brotherly concord:

"Et ipse
Notus in fratres animi paterni."[9]

We are not here to bring the love we bear to women, though it be an act of our own choice, into comparison; nor rank it with the others. The fire of this, I confess,

"Neque enim est dea nescia nostri
Quæ dulcem curis miscet amaritiem,"[10]

is more active, more eager, and more sharp: but withal, 'tis more precipitant, fickle, moving, and inconstant; a fever subject to intermissions and paroxysms, that has seized but on one part of us. Whereas in friendship, 'tis a general and universal fire, but temperate and equal, a constant established heat, all gentle and smooth, without poignancy or

---

[8] On Brotherly Love, c. 4.

[9] "And I myself noted for paternal love towards my brothers." — Horace, Ode ii. 2, 6.

[10] "Nor is the goddess unknown to me, who mixes a pleasing sorrow with my love's flame." — Catullus, lxviii. 17.

roughness. Moreover, in love, 'tis no other than frantic desire for that which flies from us:

> "Come segue la lepre il cacciatore
> Al freddo, al caldo, alla montagna, al lito;
> Ne più l' estima poi che presa vede;
> E sol dietro a chi fugge affretta il piede:"[11]

so soon as it enters into the terms of friendship, that is to say, into a concurrence of desires, it vanishes and is gone, fruition destroys it, as having only a fleshly end, and such a one as is subject to satiety. Friendship, on the contrary, is enjoyed proportionably as it is desired; and only grows up, is nourished and improves by enjoyment, as being of itself spiritual, and the soul growing still more refined by practice. Under this perfect friendship, the other fleeting affections have in my younger years found some place in me, to say nothing of him, who himself so confesses but too much in his verses; so that I had both these passions, but always so, that I could myself well enough distinguish them, and never in any degree of comparison with one another; the first maintaining its flight in so lofty and so brave a place, as with disdain to look down, and see the other flying at a far humbler pitch below.

As concerning marriage, besides that it is a covenant, the entrance into which only is free, but the continuance in it forced and compulsory, having another dependence than that of our own freewill, and a bargain commonly contracted to other ends, there almost always happens a thousand intricacies in it to unravel, enough to break the thread and to divert the current of a lively affection: whereas friendship has no manner of business or traffic with aught but itself. Moreover, to say truth, the ordinary talent of women is not such as is sufficient to maintain the conference and communication required to the support of this sacred tie; nor do they appear to be endued with constancy of mind, to sustain the pinch of so hard and durable a knot. And doubtless, if without this, there could be such a free and voluntary familiarity contracted, where not only the souls might have this entire fruition, but the bodies also might share in the alliance, and a man be engaged throughout, the friendship would certainly be more full and perfect; but it is without example that this sex has ever yet arrived at such perfection; and, by the common consent of the ancient schools, it is wholly rejected from it.

That other Grecian licence is justly abhorred by our manners; which also, from having, according to their practice, a so necessary disparity of age and difference of offices betwixt the lovers, answered no more to the perfect union and harmony that we here require, than the other: "quis est enim iste amor amicitiæ? cur neque deformem adolescentem quis-

---

[11] "As the hunter pursues the hare, through cold and heat, over hill and dale, but, so soon as it is taken, no longer cares for it, and only delights in chasing that which flees from him." —Ariosto, [Orlando Furioso,] x. 7.

quam amat, neque formosum senem?"[12] Neither will that very picture that the Academy presents of it, as I conceive, contradict me, when I say, that this first fury inspired by the son of Venus into the heart of the lover, upon sight of the flower and prime of a springing and blossoming youth, to which they allow all the insolent and passionate efforts that an immoderate ardour can produce, was simply founded upon external beauty, the false image of corporal generation; for it could not ground this love upon the soul, the sight of which as yet lay concealed, was but now springing, and not of maturity to blossom: that this fury, if it seized upon a low spirit, the means by which it preferred its suit were rich presents, favour in advancement to dignities, and such trumpery, which they by no means approve: if on a more generous soul, the pursuit was suitably generous, by philosophical instructions, precepts to revere religion, to obey the laws, to die for the good of one's country; by examples of valour, prudence, and justice, the lover studying to render himself acceptable by the grace and beauty of his soul, that of his body being long since faded and decayed, hoping by this mental society to establish a more firm and lasting contract. When this courtship came to effect in due season (for that which they do not require in the lover, namely, leisure and discretion in his pursuit, they strictly require in the person loved, forasmuch as he is to judge of an internal beauty, of difficult knowledge and abstruse discovery), then there sprung in the person loved the desire of a spiritual conception, by the mediation of a spiritual beauty. This was the principal; the corporeal, an accidental and secondary matter: quite the contrary as to the lover. For this reason they prefer the person beloved, maintaining that the gods in like manner preferred him too, and very much blame the poet Æschylus for having, in the loves of Achilles and Patroclus, given the lover's part to Achilles, who was in the first flower and pubescency of his youth, and the handsomest of all the Greeks. After this general community, the sovereign and most worthy part presiding and governing, and performing its proper offices, they say, that thence great utility was derived, both by private and public concerns: that it constituted the force and power of the countries where it prevailed, and the chiefest security of liberty and justice. Of which the salutiferous loves of Harmonius and Aristogiton are instances. And therefore it is that they called it sacred and divine, and conceive that nothing but the violence of tyrants and the baseness of the common people are inimical to it. Finally, all that can be said in favour of the Academy, is, that it was a love which ended in friendship, which well enough agrees with the Stoical definition of love: "Amorem conatum esse amicitiæ faciendæ ex pulchritudinis specie."[13]

---

[12] "For what is that love of friendship? why does no one love a deformed youth, or a comely old man?" — Cicero, Tusc. Quæs., iv. 33.

[13] "Love is a desire of contracting friendship arising from the beauty of the object." — Cicero, Tusc. Quæs., vi. 34.

I return to my own more just and true description. "Omnino amicitiæ, corroboratis jam confirmatisque, et ingeniis, et ætatibus,
judicandæ sunt."[14] For the rest, what we commonly call friends and
friendships, are nothing but acquaintance and familiarities, either occa-
sionally contracted, or upon some design, by means of which there
happens some little intercourse betwixt our souls. But in the friendship I
speak of, they mix and work themselves into one piece, with so universal
a mixture, that there is no more sign of the seam by which they were first
conjoined. If a man should importune me to give a reason why I loved
him, I find it could no otherwise be expressed, than by making answer:
because it was he, because it was I. There is, beyond all that I am able to
say, I know not what inexplicable and fated power that brought on this
union. We sought one another long before we met, and by the charac-
ters we heard of one another, which wrought upon our affections more
than, in reason, mere reports should do; I think 'twas by some secret
appointment of heaven. We embraced in our names; and at our first
meeting, which was accidentally at a great city entertainment, we found
ourselves so mutually taken with one another, so acquainted, and so
endeared betwixt ourselves, that from thenceforward nothing was so
near to us as one another. He wrote an excellent Latin satire, since
printed, wherein he excuses the precipitation of our intelligence, so
suddenly come to perfection, saying, that destined to have so short a
continuance, as begun so late (for we were both full-grown men, and he
some years the older), there was no time to lose, nor were we tied to
conform to the example of those slow and regular friendships, that
require so many precautions of long preliminary conversation. This has
no other idea than that of itself, and can only refer to itself: this is no one
special consideration, nor two, nor three, nor four, nor a thousand; 'tis I
know not what quintessence of all this mixture, which, seizing my whole
will, carried it to plunge and lose itself in his, and that having seized his
whole will, brought it back with equal concurrence and appetite to
plunge and lose itself in mine. I may truly say lose, reserving nothing to
ourselves, that was either his or mine.

When Lælius,[15] in the presence of the Roman consuls, who after they
had sentenced Tiberius Gracchus, prosecuted all those who had had
any familiarity with him also, came to ask Caius Blosius, who was his
chiefest friend, how much he would have done for him, and that he
made answer: "All things." "How! All things!" said Lælius. "And what if
he had commanded you to fire our temples?" "He would never have
commanded me that," replied Blosius. "But what if he had?" said
Lælius. "I would have obeyed him," said the other. If he was so perfect a

---

[14] "Those are only to be reputed friendships, that are fortified and confirmed by judgment
and length of time." — Cicero, De Amicit., c. 20.

[15] Cicero, De Amicit., c. 11.

friend to Gracchus, as the histories report him to have been, there was yet no necessity of offending the consuls by such a bold confession, though he might still have retained the assurance he had of Gracchus' disposition. However, those who accuse this answer as seditious, do not well understand the mystery; nor presuppose, as it was true, that he had Gracchus' will in his sleeve, both by the power of a friend, and the perfect knowledge he had of the man: they were more friends than citizens, more friends to one another than either friends or enemies to their country, or than friends to ambition and innovation; having absolutely given up themselves to one another, either held absolutely the reins of the other's inclination; and suppose all this guided by virtue, and all this by the conduct of reason, which also without these it had not been possible to do, Blosius' answer was such as it ought to be. If any of their actions flew out of the handle, they were neither (according to my measure of friendship) friends to one another, nor to themselves. As to the rest, this answer carries no worse sound, than mine would do to one that should ask me: "If your will should command you to kill your daughter, would you do it?" and that I should make answer, that I would; for this expresses no consent to such an act, forasmuch as I do not in the least suspect my own will, and as little that of such a friend. 'Tis not in the power of all the eloquence in the world, to dispossess me of the certainty I have of the intentions and resolutions of my friend; nay, no one action of his, what face soever it might bear, could be presented to me, of which I could not presently, and at first sight, find out the moving cause. Our souls had drawn so unanimously together, they had considered each other with so ardent an affection, and with the like affection laid open the very bottom of our hearts to one another's view, that I not only knew his as well as my own; but should certainly in any concern of mine have trusted my interest much more willingly with him, than with myself.

Let no one, therefore, rank other common friendships with such a one as this. I have had as much experience of these, as another, and of the most perfect of their kind: but I do not advise that any should confound the rules of the one and the other, for they would find themselves much deceived. In those other ordinary friendships, you are to walk with bridle in your hand, with prudence and circumspection, for in them the knot is not so sure, that a man may not half suspect it will slip. "Love him," said Chilo,[16] "so, as if you were one day to hate him; and hate him so, as you were one day to love him." This precept, though abominable in the sovereign and perfect friendship I speak of, is nevertheless very sound, as to the practice of the ordinary and customary ones, and to which the saying that Aristotle had so frequent in his

---

[16] Aulus Gellius, i. 3.

mouth, "O my friends, there is no friend;"[17] may very fitly be applied. In this noble commerce, good offices, presents, and benefits, by which other friendships are supported and maintained, do not deserve so much as to be mentioned; and the reason is the concurrence of our wills; for, as the kindness I have for myself, receives no increase, for anything I relieve myself withal in time of need (whatever the Stoics say), and as I do not find myself obliged to myself for any service I do myself: so the union of such friends, being truly perfect, deprives them of all idea of such duties, and makes them loathe and banish from their conversation these words of division and distinction, benefit, obligation, acknowledgment, entreaty, thanks, and the like. All things, wills, thoughts, opinions, goods, wives, children, honours, and lives, being in effect common betwixt them, and that absolute concurrence of affections being no other than one soul in two bodies (according to that very proper definition of Aristotle),[18] they can neither lend nor give anything to one another. This is the reason why the lawgivers, to honour marriage with some resemblance of this divine alliance, interdict all gifts betwixt man and wife; inferring by that, that all should belong to each of them, and that they have nothing to divide or to give to each other.

If, in the friendship of which I speak, one could give to the other, the receiver of the benefit would be the man that obliged his friend; for each of them contending and above all things studying how to be useful to the other, he that administers the occasion is the liberal man, in giving his friend the satisfaction of doing that towards him, which above all things he most desires. When the philosopher Diogenes wanted money, he used to say,[19] that he redemanded it of his friends, not that he demanded it. And to let you see the practical working of this, I will here produce an ancient and singular example;[20] Eudamidas a Corinthian, had two friends, Charixenus a Sycionian, and Areteus a Corinthian; this man coming to die, being poor, and his two friends rich, he made his will after this manner. "I bequeath to Areteus the maintenance of my mother, to support and provide for her in her old age; and to Charixenus I bequeath the care of marrying my daughter, and to give her as good a portion as he is able; and in case one of these chance to die, I hereby substitute the survivor in his place." They who first saw this will, made themselves very merry at the contents: but the legatees being made acquainted with it, accepted it with very great content; and one of them, Charixenus, dying within five days after, and Areteus, by that means, having the charge of both duties devolved solely to him, he nourished

---

[17] Diogenes Laertius, v. 21.

[18] Idem, v. 20.

[19] Diogenes Laertius, vi. 46.

[20] From the "Toxaris" of Lucian, c. 22.

the old woman with very great care and tenderness, and of five talents he had in estate, he gave two and a half in marriage with an only daughter he had of his own, and two and a half in marriage with the daughter of Eudamidas, and in one and the same day solemnised both their nuptials.

This example is very full, if one thing were not to be objected, namely, the multitude of friends: for the perfect friendship I speak of is indivisible; each one gives himself so entirely to his friend, that he has nothing left to distribute to others: on the contrary, is sorry that he is not double, treble, or quadruple, and that he has not many souls, and many wills, to confer them all upon this one object. Common friendships will admit of division; one may love the beauty of this person, the good-humour of that, the liberality of a third, the paternal affection of a fourth, the fraternal love of a fifth, and so of the rest: but this friendship that possesses the whole soul, and there rules and sways with an absolute sovereignty, cannot possibly admit of a rival. If two at the same time should call to you for succour, to which of them would you run? Should they require of you contrary offices, how could you serve them both? Should one commit a thing to your silence, that it were of importance to the other to know, how would you disengage yourself? A unique and particular friendship dissolves all other obligations whatsoever: the secret I have sworn not to reveal to any other, I may without perjury communicate to him who is not another, but myself. 'Tis miracle enough certainly, for a man to double himself, and those that talk of tripling, talk they know not of what. Nothing is extreme, that has its like; and he who shall suppose, that of two, I love one as much as the other, that they mutually love one another too, and love me as much as I love them, multiplies into a confraternity the most single of units, and whereof, moreover, one alone is the hardest thing in the world to find. The rest of this story suits very well with what I was saying; for Eudamidas, as a bounty and favour, bequeaths to his friends a legacy of employing themselves in his necessity; he leaves them heirs to this liberality of his, which consists in giving them the opportunity of conferring a benefit upon him; and doubtless, the force of friendship is more eminently apparent in this act of his, than in that of Areteus. In short, these are effects not to be imagined nor comprehended by such as have not experience of them, and which make me infinitely honour and admire the answer of that young soldier to Cyrus, by whom being asked how much he would take for a horse, with which he had won the prize of a race, and whether he would exchange him for a kingdom? "No, truly, sir," said he, "but I would give him with all my heart, to get thereby a true friend, could I find out any man worthy of that alliance."[21] He did not say ill in saying, "could I find:" for though one may almost every-

---

[21] Xenophon, Cyropædia, viii. 3.

where meet with men sufficiently qualified for a superficial acquaintance, yet in this, where a man is to deal from the very bottom of his
heart, without any manner of reservation, it will be requisite, that all the
wards and springs be truly wrought, and perfectly sure.

In confederations that hold but by one end, we are only to provide
against the imperfections, that particularly concern that end. It can be of
no importance to me of what religion my physician or my lawyer is; this
consideration has nothing in common with the offices of friendship
which they owe me; and I am of the same indifference in the domestic
acquaintance my servants must necessarily contract with me. I never
inquire, when I am to take a footman, if he be chaste, but if he be
diligent; and am not solicitous if my muleteer be given to gaming, as if
he be strong and able; or if my cook be a swearer, if he be a good cook. I
do not take upon me to direct what other men should do in the
government of their families, there are plenty that meddle enough with
that, but only give an account of my method in my own.

> "Mihi sic usus est: tibi, ut opus est facto, face."[22]

For table-talk, I prefer the pleasant and witty before the learned and
the grave; in bed, beauty before goodness; in common discourse, the
ablest speaker, whether or no there be sincerity in the case. And, as he
that was found astride upon a hobby-horse, playing with his children,
entreated the person who had surprised him in that posture, to say
nothing of it till himself came to be a father,[23] supposing that the
fondness that would then possess his own soul, would render him a
fairer judge of such an action; so I, also, could wish to speak to such as
have had experience of what I say: though, knowing how remote a thing
such a friendship is from the common practice, and how rarely it is to be
found, I despair of meeting with any such judge. For even these discourses left us by antiquity upon this subject, seem to me flat and poor,
in comparison of the sense I have of it, and in this particular, the effects
surpass even the precepts of philosophy.

> "Nil ego contulerim jucundo sanus amico."[24]

The ancient Menander declared him to be happy that had had the
good fortune to meet with but the shadow of a friend:[25] and doubtless he
had good reason to say so, especially if he spoke by experience: for in

---

[22] "This has been my way; as for you, do as you think fit." — Terence, Heaut., i. 1, 28.

[23] Plutarch, Life of Agesilaus, c. 9.

[24] "While I have sense left to me, there will never be anything more acceptable to me than
an agreeable friend." — Horace, Sat., i. 5, 44.

[25] Plutarch on Brotherly Love, c. 3.

good earnest, if I compare all the rest of my life, though, thanks be to God, I have passed my time pleasantly enough, and at my ease, and the loss of such a friend excepted, free from any grievous affliction, and in great tranquillity of mind, having been contented with my natural and original commodities, without being solicitous after others; if I should compare it all, I say, with the four years I had the happiness to enjoy the sweet society of this excellent man, 'tis nothing but smoke, an obscure and tedious night. From the day that I lost him,

> "Quem semper acerbum,
> Semper honoratum (sic, dî, voluistis) habebo,"[26]

I have only led a languishing life; and the very pleasures that present themselves to me, instead of administering anything of consolation, double my affliction for his loss. We were halves throughout, and to that degree, that methinks, by outliving him, I defraud him of his part.

> "Nec fas esse ulla me voluptate hic frui
> Decrevi, tantisper dum ille abest meus particeps."[27]

I was so grown and accustomed to be always his double in all places and in all things, that methinks I am no more than half of myself.

> "Illam meæ si partem animæ tulit
> Maturior vis, quid moror altera?
> Nec carus æque, nec superstes
> Integer? Ille dies utramque
> Duxit ruinam."[28]

There is no action or imagination of mine wherein I do not miss him; as I know that he would have missed me: for as he surpassed me by infinite degrees in virtue and all other accomplishments, so he also did in the duties of friendship.

> "Quis desiderio sit pudor, aut modus
> Tam cari capitis?"[29]

> "O misero frater adempte mihi!
> Omnia tecum una perierunt gaudia nostra,

---

[26] "A day to me for ever sad, for ever sacred, so have you willed, ye gods." — Æneid, v. 49.

[27] "I have determined that it will never be right for me to enjoy any pleasure, so long as he, with whom I shared in all pleasures, is away." — Terence, Heaut., i. 1, 97.

[28] "If that half of my soul were snatched away from me by an untimely stroke, why should the other stay? That which remains will not be equally dear, will not be a whole: the same day will involve the destruction of both." — Horace, Ode ii. 17, 5.

[29] "What shame can there be, or measure, in lamenting so dear a friend?" — Horace, Ode i. 24, 1.

Quæ tuus in vita dulcis alebat amor.
Tu mea, tu moriens fregisti commoda, frater;
  Tecum una tota est nostra sepulta anima:
Cujus ego interitu tota de mente fugavi
  Hæc studia, atque omnes delicias animi.
Alloquar? audiero nunquam tua verba loquentem?
  Nunquam ego te, vita frater amabilior
Aspiciam posthac; at certe semper amabo;"[30]

But let us hear a boy of sixteen speak.[31]

"Because I have found that that work has been since brought out, and with a mischievous design, by those who aim at disturbing and changing the condition of our government, without troubling themselves to think whether they are likely to improve it: and because they have mixed up his work with some of their own performance, I have refrained from inserting it here. But that the memory of the author may not be injured, nor suffer with such as could not come near hand to be acquainted with his principles, I here give them to understand, that it was written by him in his boyhood, and that by way of exercise only, as a common theme that has been tumbled and tossed by a thousand writers. I make no question, but that he himself believed what he wrote, being so conscientious that he would not so much as lie in jest: and I moreover know, that could it have been in his own choice, he had rather have been born at Venice, than at Sarlac, and he had reason. But he had another maxim sovereignly imprinted in his soul, very religiously to obey and submit to the laws under which he was born. There never was a better citizen, more affectionate to his country; nor a greater enemy to all the commotions and innovations of his time: so that he would much rather have employed his talent to the extinguishing of those civil flames, than have added any fuel to them; he had a mind fashioned to the model of better ages. But in exchange of this serious piece, I will present you with another of a more gay and frolic air, from the same hand, and written at the same age."

---

[30] "O brother, taken from me miserable! with thee, all our joys have vanished, those joys which, in thy life, thy dear love nourished. Dying, thou, my brother, hast destroyed all my happiness. My whole soul is buried with thee. Thou dead, I have bidden adieu to the Muses, to all the studies which charmed my mind. No more can I speak to thee; no more hear thy voice. Never again shall I see thee, O brother dearer to me than life. Nought remains, but that I love thee while life shall endure."—Catullus, lxviii. 20; lxv. 9.

[31] In Cotton's translation, the work referred to is "those Memoirs upon the famous edict of January," of which mention has already been made in the present edition [see note 4, above]. The edition of 1580, however, and the Variorum edition of Louandre, which has been here adopted, indicate no particular work; but the edition of 1580 has it "this boy of eighteen years" (which was the age at which La Boetie wrote his "Servitude Volontaire"), and speaks of "a boy of sixteen" as occurring only in the common editions, and it would seem tolerably clear that this more important work was, in fact, the production to which Montaigne refers, and that the proper reading of the text should be "eighteen years."

Of Solitude

LET US pretermit that long comparison betwixt the active and the solitary life; and as for the fine saying with which ambition and avarice palliate their vices, that we are not born for ourselves but for the public,[1] let us boldly appeal to those who are in public affairs; let them lay their hands upon their hearts, and then say whether, on the contrary, they do not rather aspire to titles and offices and that tumult of the world to make their private advantage at the public expense. The corrupt ways by which in this our time they arrive at the height to which their ambitions aspire, manifestly enough declares that their ends cannot be very good. Let us tell ambition, that it is she herself who gives us a taste of solitude; for what does she so much avoid as society? What does she so much seek as elbow-room. A man may do well or ill everywhere: but if what Bias says be true,[2] that the greatest part is the worse part, or what the Preacher says: there is not one good of a thousand;

> "Rari quippe boni: numero vix sunt totidem quot
> Thebarum portæ, vel divitis ostia Nili,"[3]

the contagion is very dangerous in the crowd. A man must either imitate the vicious or hate them: both are dangerous things, either to resemble them because they are many or to hate many because they are unresembling to ourselves.[4] Merchants who go to sea are in the right, when they are cautious that those who embark with them in the same bottom, be neither dissolute blasphemers nor vicious other ways, looking upon such society as unfortunate. And therefore it was that Bias pleasantly said to some, who being with him in a dangerous storm implored the assistance of the gods: "Peace, speak softly," said he, "that they may not know you

---

[1] This is the eulogium passed by Lucan on Cato of Utica, ii. 383.

[2] Diogenes Laertius, in vitâ [i.e., in his "Life of Bias"].

[3] "Good men are scarce: we could hardly reckon up as many as there are gates to Thebes, or mouths to the Nile." — Juvenal, Sat., xiii. 26.

[4] Seneca, Ep., 7.

are here in my company."[5] And of more pressing example, Albuquerque, viceroy in the Indies for Emmanuel King of Portugal, in an extreme peril of shipwreck, took a young boy upon his shoulders, for this only end that, in the society of their common danger, his innocence might serve to protect him, and to recommend him to the divine favour, that they might get safe to shore. 'Tis not that a wise man may not live everywhere content, and be alone in the very crowd of a palace: but if it be left to his own choice, the schoolman will tell you that he should fly the very sight of the crowd: he will endure it, if need be; but, if it be referred to him, he will choose to be alone. He cannot think himself sufficiently rid of vice, if he must yet contend with it in other men. Charondas punished those as evil men who were convicted of keeping ill company.[6] There is nothing so unsociable and sociable as man, the one by his vice, the other by his nature. And Antisthenes, in my opinion, did not give him a satisfactory answer, who reproached him with frequenting ill company, by saying that the physicians lived well enough amongst the sick:[7] for if they contribute to the health of the sick, no doubt but by the contagion, continual sight of, and familiarity with diseases, they must of necessity impair their own.

Now the end, I take it, is all one, to live at more leisure and at one's ease: but men do not always take the right way. They often think they have totally taken leave of all business, when they have only exchanged one employment for another: there is little less trouble in governing a private family than a whole kingdom. Wherever the mind is perplexed, it is in an entire disorder, and domestic employments are not less troublesome for being less important. Moreover, for having shaken off the court and the exchange, we have not taken leave of the principal vexations of life:

"Ratio et prudentia curas,
Non locus effusi late maris arbiter, aufert;"[8]

ambition, avarice, irresolution, fear, and inordinate desires, do not leave us because we forsake our native country:

"Et
Post equitem sedet atra cura;"[9]

they often follow us even to cloisters and philosophical schools; nor deserts, nor caves, hair-shirts, nor fasts, can disengage us from them:

---

[5] Diogenes Laertius, in vitâ.

[6] Diodorus Siculus, xii. 4.

[7] Diogenes Laertius, Life of Antisthenes.

[8] "Reason and prudence, not a place with a commanding view of the great ocean, banish care." — Horace, Ep., i. 2.

[9] "Black care sits behind the horseman." — Horace, Od., iii. 1, 40.

"Hæret lateri lethalis arundo."[10]

One telling Socrates, that such a one was nothing improved by his travels: "I very well believe it," said he, "for he took himself along with him."[11]

> "Quid terras alio calentes
> Sole mutamus? patriæ quis exsul
> Se quoque fugit?"[12]

If a man do not first discharge both himself and his mind of the burden with which he finds himself oppressed, motion will but make it press the harder and sit the heavier, as the lading of a ship is of less encumbrance when fast and bestowed in a settled posture. You do a sick man more harm than good in removing him from place to place; you fix and establish the disease by motion, as stakes sink deeper and more firmly into the earth by being moved up and down in the place where they are designed to stand. Therefore, it is not enough to get remote from the public; 'tis not enough to shift the soil only; a man must flee from the popular conditions that have taken possession of his soul, he must sequester and come again to himself.

> "Rupi jam vincula, dicas:
> Nam luctata canis nodum arripit; attamen illi,
> Quum fugit, a collo trahitur pars longa catenæ."[13]

We still carry our fetters along with us. 'Tis not an absolute liberty; we yet cast back a look upon what we have left behind us; the fancy is still full of it:

> "Nisi purgatum est pectus, quæ prælia nobis
> Atque pericula tunc ingratis insinuandum?
> Quantæ conscindunt hominem cupedinis acres
> Sollicitum curæ? quantique perinde timores?
> Quidve superbia, spurcitia, ac petulantia, quantas
> Efficiunt clades? quid luxus, desidiesque?"[14]

---

[10] "The fatal shaft sticks in the wounded side." — Æneid, iv. 73.

[11] Seneca, Ep., 104.

[12] "Why do we seek climates warmed by another sun? Who is the man that by fleeing from his country, can also flee from himself?" — Horace, Od., ii. 16, 18.

[13] "You say, perhaps, you have broken your chain: the dog who after long efforts has broken his chain, still in his flight drags a heavy portion of it after him." — Persius, Sat., v. 158.

[14] "But unless the mind is purified, what internal combats and dangers must we incur in spite of all our efforts! How many bitter anxieties, how many terrors, follow upon unregulated passion! What destruction befals us from pride, lust, petulant anger! What evils arise from luxury and sloth!" — Lucretius, v. 4.

Our disease lies in the mind, which cannot escape from itself;

"In culpa est animus, qui se non effugit unquam,"[15]

and therefore is to be called home and confined within itself: that is the
true solitude, and that may be enjoyed even in populous cities and the
courts of kings, though more commodiously apart.

Now, since we will attempt to live alone, and to waive all manner of
conversation amongst men, let us so order it that our content may
depend wholly upon ourselves; let us dissolve all obligations that ally us
to others; let us obtain this from ourselves, that we may live alone in
good earnest, and live at our ease too.

Stilpo having escaped from the fire that consumed the city where he
lived, and wherein he had lost his wife, children, goods, and all that ever
he was master of, Demetrius Poliorcetes seeing him, in so great a ruin of
his country, appear with a serene and undisturbed countenance, asked
him if he had received no loss? To which he made answer, No; and that,
thanks be to God, nothing was lost of his.[16] This also was the meaning of
the philosopher Antisthenes, when he pleasantly said, that "men should
furnish themselves with such things as would float, and might with the
owner escape the storm;"[17] and certainly a wise man never loses anything if he have himself. When the city of Nola was ruined by the
barbarians, Paulinus, who was bishop of that place, having there lost all
he had, and himself a prisoner, prayed after this manner: "O Lord,
defend me from being sensible of this loss; for Thou knowest they have
yet touched nothing of that which is mine."[18] The riches that made him
rich and the goods that made him good, were still kept entire. This it is
to make choice of treasures that can secure themselves from plunder
and violence, and to hide them in such a place into which no one can
enter and that is not to be betrayed by any but ourselves. Wives, children, and goods must be had, and especially health, by him that can get
it; but we are not so to set our hearts upon them that our happiness must
have its dependence upon them; we must reserve a backshop, wholly
our own and entirely free, wherein to settle our true liberty, our principal
solitude and retreat. And in this we must for the most part entertain
ourselves with ourselves, and so privately that no exotic knowledge or
communication be admitted there; there to laugh and to talk, as if
without wife, children, goods, train, or attendance, to the end, that when
it shall so fall out that we must lose any or all of these, it may be no new
thing to be without them. We have a mind pliable in itself, that will be

---

15 Horace, Ep., i. 14, 13. The citation is translated in the preceding passage.
16 Seneca, Ep., 7.
17 Diogenes Laertius, vi. 6.
18 St. Augustin, De Civit. Dei, i. 10.

company; that has wherewithal to attack and to defend, to receive and to give: let us not then fear in this solitude to languish under an uncomfortable vacuity.

"In solis sis tibi turba locis."[19]

Virtue is satisfied with herself, without discipline, without words, without effects. In our ordinary actions there is not one of a thousand that concerns ourselves. He that thou seest scrambling up the ruins of that wall, furious and transported, against whom so many harquebuss-shots are levelled; and that other all over scars, pale, and fainting with hunger, and yet resolved rather to die than to open the gates to him; dost thou think that these men are there upon their own account? No; peradventure in the behalf of one whom they never saw and who never concerns himself for their pains and danger, but lies wallowing the while in sloth and pleasure: this other slavering, blear-eyed, slovenly fellow, that thou seest come out of his study after midnight, dost thou think he has been tumbling over books, to learn how to become a better man, wiser, and more content? No such matter; he will there end his days, but he will teach posterity the measure of Plautus' verses and the true orthography of a Latin word. Who is it that does not voluntarily exchange his health, his repose, and his very life for reputation and glory, the most useless, frivolous, and false coin that passes current amongst us. Our own death does not sufficiently terrify and trouble us; let us, moreover, charge ourselves with those of our wives, children, and family: our own affairs do not afford us anxiety enough; let us undertake those of our neighbours and friends, still more to break our brains and torment us.

"Vah! quemquamne hominem in animum instituere, aut
Parare, quod sit carius, quam ipse est sibi?"[20]

Solitude seems to me to wear the best favour, in such as have already employed their most active and flourishing age in the world's service; after the example of Thales. We have lived enough for others, let us at least live out the small remnant of life for ourselves; let us now call in our thoughts and intentions to ourselves, and to our own ease and repose. 'Tis no light thing to make a sure retreat; it will be enough for us to do without mixing other enterprises. Since God gives us leisure to order our removal, let us make ready, truss our baggage, take leave betimes of the company, and disentangle ourselves from those violent importunities that engage us elsewhere and separate us from ourselves.

---

[19] "In solitude, be company for thyself." — Tibullus, vi. 13, 12.

[20] "Ah! can any man discover or devise anything dearer than he is to himself?" — Terence, Adel., i. 1, 13.

We must break the knot of our obligations, how strong soever, and hereafter love this or that, but espouse nothing, but ourselves: that is to say, let the remainder be our own, but not so joined and so close as not to be forced away without flaying us or tearing out part of our whole. The greatest thing in the world is for a man to know that he is his own. 'Tis time to wean ourselves from society, when we can no longer add anything to it; he who is not in a condition to lend must forbid himself to borrow. Our forces begin to fail us: let us call them in and concentrate them in and for ourselves. He that can cast off within himself and resolve the offices of friendship and company, let him do it. In this decay of nature which renders him useless, burdensome and importunate to others, let him take care not to be useless, burdensome and importunate to himself. Let him soothe and caress himself, and above all things be sure to govern himself with reverence to his reason and conscience to that degree as to be ashamed to make a false step in their presence. "Rarum est enim, ut satis se quisque vereatur."[21] Socrates[22] says, that boys are to cause themselves to be instructed, men to exercise themselves in well-doing, and old men to retire from all civil and military employments, living at their own discretion, without the obligation to any office. There are some complexions more proper for these precepts of retirement than others. Such as are of a soft and dull apprehension, and of a tender will and affection not readily to be subdued or employed, whereof I am one, both by natural condition and by reflection, will sooner incline to this advice, than active and busy souls, which embrace all, engage in all, are hot upon everything, which offer, present, and give themselves up to every occasion. We are to use these accidental and extraneous commodities, so far as they are pleasant to us, but by no means to lay our principal foundation there; 'tis no true one; neither nature nor reason allows it so to be. Why therefore should we, contrary to their laws, enslave our own contentment to the power of another? To anticipate also the accidents of fortune, to deprive ourselves of the conveniences we have in our own power, as several have done upon the account of devotion, and some philosophers by reasoning; to be one's own servant, to lie hard, to put out our own eyes, to throw our wealth into the river, to seek out grief; these, by the misery of this life, aiming at bliss in another; those, by laying themselves low to avoid the danger of falling: all such are acts of an excessive virtue. The stoutest and most resolute natures render even their hiding away glorious and exemplary:

---

[21] "For 'tis rarely seen that men have respect and reverence enough for themselves." — Quintilian, x. 7.

[22] Stobæus, Serm. xli.

"Tuta et parvula laudo,
Quum res dificiunt, satis inter vilia fortis:
Verum, ubi quid melius contingit et unctius, idem
Hos sapere, et solos aio bene vivere, quorum
Conspicitur nitidis fundata pecunia villis."[23]

A great deal less would serve my turn well enough. 'Tis enough for me, under fortune's favour, to prepare myself for her disgrace, and, being at my ease, to represent to myself, as far as my imagination can stretch, the ill to come; as we do at jousts and tiltings, where we counterfeit war in the greatest calm of peace. I do not think Arcesilaus the philosopher the less temperate and virtuous, for knowing that he made use of gold and silver vessels, when the condition of his fortune allowed him so to do;[24] I have indeed a better opinion of him, than if he had denied himself what he used with liberality and moderation. I see the utmost limits of natural necessity: and considering a poor man begging at my door, ofttimes more jocund and more healthy than I myself am, I put myself into his place, and attempt to dress my mind after his mode; and running, in like manner, over other examples, though I fancy death, poverty, contempt, and sickness treading on my heels, I easily resolve not to be affrighted, forasmuch as a less than I takes them with so much patience; and am not willing to believe that a less understanding can do more than a greater, or that the effects of precept cannot arrive to as great a height as those of custom. And knowing of how uncertain duration these accidental conveniences are, I never forget, in the height of all my enjoyments, to make it my chiefest prayer to Almighty God, that He will please to render me content with myself and the condition wherein I am. I see young men very gay and frolic, who nevertheless keep a mass of pills in their trunk at home, to take when they've got a cold, which they fear so much the less, because they think they have remedy at hand. Every one should do in like manner, and, moreover, if they find themselves subject to some more violent disease, should furnish themselves with such medicines as may numb and stupefy the part.

The employment a man should choose for such a life, ought neither to be a laborious nor an unpleasing one; otherwise 'tis to no purpose at all to be retired. And this depends upon every one's liking and humour. Mine has no manner of complacency for husbandry, and such as love it ought to apply themselves to it with moderation.

---

[23] "When I run short, I laud a humble and safe condition, content with little: when things turn round, then I change my note, and say that none are wise or know how to live, but those who have plenty of money to lay out in shining villas." — Horace, Ep., i. 15, 42.

[24] Diogenes Laertius, iv. 38.

"Conentur sibi res, non se submittere rebus."[25]

Husbandry is otherwise a very servile employment, as Sallust calls it;[26] though some parts of it are more excusable than the rest, as the care of gardens, which Xenophon attributes to Cyrus;[27] and a mean may be found out betwixt the sordid and low application, so full of perpetual solicitude, which is seen in men who make it their entire business and study, and the stupid and extreme negligence, letting all things go at random, which we see in others:

> "Democriti pecus edit agellos
> Cultaque, dum peregre est animus sine corpore velox."[28]

But let us hear what advice the younger Pliny[29] gives his friend Caninius Rufus upon the subject of solitude: "I advise thee, in the full and plentiful retirement wherein thou art, to leave to thy hinds the care of thy husbandry, and to addict thyself to the study of letters, to extract from thence something that may be entirely and absolutely thine own." By which, he means reputation; like Cicero, who says, that he would employ his solitude and retirement from public affairs, to acquire by his writings an immortal life.[30]

> "Usque adeone
> Scire tuum, nihil est, nisi te scire hoc, sciat alter?"[31]

It appears to be reason, when a man talks of retiring from the world, that he should look quite out of himself. These do it but by halves: they design well enough for themselves when they shall be no more in it; but still they pretend to extract the fruits of that design from the world, when absent from it, by a ridiculous contradiction.

The imagination of those who seek solitude upon the account of devotion, filling their hopes and courage with certainty of divine promises in the other life, is much more rationally founded. They propose to

---

[25] "Endeavour to make circumstances subject to me, and not me subject to circumstances." — Horace, Ep., i. 1, 19, whose text, however, is, "Et mihi res, non me rebus, subjungere conor."

[26] Catiline, c. 4.

[27] Economics, iv. 20.

[28] "Democritus' cattle eat his corn and spoil his fields, whilst his mind ranges abroad without the body." — Horace, Ep., i. 12, 12.

[29] Ep., i. 3.

[30] Cicero, Orator., c. 43.

[31] "Is all thy learning nothing, unless another knows that thou knowest?" — Persius, Sat., i. 23.

themselves God, an infinite object in goodness and power; the soul has there wherewithal, at full liberty, to satiate her desires: afflictions and sufferings turn to their advantage, being undergone for the acquisition of eternal health and joy; death is to be wished and longed for, where it is the passage to so perfect a condition; the asperity of the rules they impose upon themselves is immediately softened by custom, and all their carnal appetites baffled and subdued, by refusing to humour and feed them, these being only supported by use and exercise. This sole end therefore of another happy and immortal life is that, which really merits that we should abandon the pleasures and conveniences of this; and he who can really and constantly inflame his soul with the ardour of this vivid faith and hope, erects for himself in solitude a more voluptuous and delicious life than any other sort of living whatever.

Neither the end then nor the means of this advice,[32] pleases me, for we often fall out of the frying-pan into the fire. This book employment is as painful as any other, and as great an enemy to health, which ought to be the first thing considered; neither ought a man to be allured with the pleasure of it, which is the same that destroys the frugal, the avaricious, the voluptuous, and the ambitious man.[33] The sages give us caution enough to beware the treachery of our desires, and to distinguish true and entire pleasures from such as are mixed and complicated with greater pain. For the most of our pleasures, say they, wheedle and caress only to strangle us, like those thieves the Egyptians called Philistæ; if the headache should come before drunkenness, we should have a care of drinking too much: but pleasure, to deceive us, marches before and conceals her train. Books are pleasant, but if, by being over-studious, we impair our health and spoil our good-humour, the best pieces we have, let us give it over; I, for my part, am one of those who think, that no fruit derived from them can recompense so great a loss. As men who have long felt themselves weakened by indisposition, give themselves up at last to the mercy of medicine and submit to certain rules of living, which they are for the future never to transgress; so he who retires, weary of and disgusted with the common way of living, ought to model this new one he enters into by the rules of reason, and to institute and establish it by premeditation and reflection. He ought to have taken leave of all sorts of labour, what advantage soever it may promise, and generally to have shaken off all those passions which disturb the tranquillity of body and soul, and then choose the way that best suits with his own humour:

---

[32] Of Pliny to Rufus.

[33] "This plodding occupation of bookes is as painfull as any other, and as great an enemie vnto health, which ought principally to be considered. And a man should not suffer him selfe to be inveagled by the pleasure he takes in them." — Florio, edit. 1613, p. 122.

"Unusquisque sua noverit ire via."[34]

In husbandry, study, hunting, and all other exercises, men are to proceed to the utmost limits of pleasure, but must take heed of engaging
further, where trouble begins to mix with it. We are to reserve so much
employment only as is necessary to keep us in breath and to defend us
from the inconveniences that the other extreme of a dull and stupid
laziness brings along with it. There are sterile knotty sciences, chiefly
hammered out for the crowd; let such be left to them who are engaged
in the world's service. I for my part care for no other books, but either
such as are pleasant and easy, to amuse me, or those that comfort and
instruct me how to regulate my life and death:

"Tacitum sylvas inter reptare salubres,
Curantem, quidquid dignum sapienti bonoque est."[35]

Wiser men, having great force and vigour of soul, may propose to
themselves a rest wholly spiritual: but for me, who have a very ordinary
soul, it is very necessary to support myself with bodily conveniences; and
age having of late deprived me of those pleasures that were more
acceptable to me, I instruct and whet my appetite to those that remain,
more suitable to this other season. We ought to hold with all our force,
both of hands and teeth, the use of the pleasures of life that our years,
one after another, snatch away from us.

"Carpamus dulcia; nostrum est,
Quod vivis; cinis, et manes, et fabula fies."[36]

Now, as to the end that Pliny and Cicero propose to us, of glory; 'tis
infinitely wide of my account. Ambition is of all others the most contrary
humour to solitude; glory and repose are things that cannot possibly
inhabit in one and the same place. For so much as I understand, these
have only their arms and legs disengaged from the crowd; their soul and
intention remain engaged behind more than ever:

"Tun', vetule, auriculis alienis colligis escas?"[37]

---

[34] Propertius, lib. ii. 25, 38. Montaigne translates the passage in the preceding paragraph.

[35] "Silently meditating in the healthy groves, what best becomes a wise and honest man." —
Horace, Ep., i. 4, 4.

[36] "Let us pluck life's sweets, 'tis for them we live: by-and-by we shall be ashes, a ghost, a
mere subject of talk." — Persius, Sat., v. 151.

[37] "Dost thou, old man, collect food for others' ears?" — Persius, Sat., i. 22.

they have only retired to take a better leap, and by a stronger motion to give a brisker charge into the crowd. Will you see how they shoot short? Let us put into the counterpoise the advice of two philosophers,[38] of two very different sects, writing, the one to Idomeneus, the other to Lucilius, their friends, to retire into solitude from worldly honours and affairs. "You have," say they, "hitherto lived swimming and floating; come now, and die in the harbour: you have given the first part of your life to the light, give what remains to the shade. It is impossible to give over business, if you do not also quit the fruit; therefore disengage yourselves from all concern of name and glory; 'tis to be feared the lustre of your former actions will give you but too much light, and follow you into your most private retreat. Quit with other pleasures that which proceeds from the approbation of another man: and as to your knowledge and parts, never concern yourselves; they will not lose their effect if yourselves be the better for them. Remember him, who being asked why he took so much pains in an art that could come to the knowledge of but few persons? 'A few are enough for me,' replied he; 'I have enough with one, I have enough with never an one.'[39] He said true; you and a companion are theatre enough to one another, or you to yourself. Let the people be to you one, and be you one to the whole people.[40] 'Tis an unworthy ambition to think to derive glory from a man's sloth and privacy: you are to do like the beasts of chase, who efface the track at the entrance into their den.[41] You are no more to concern yourself how the world talks of you, but how you are to talk to yourself. Retire yourself into yourself, but first prepare yourself there to receive yourself: it were a folly to trust yourself in your own hands, if you cannot govern yourself.[42] A man may miscarry alone as well as in company. Till you have rendered yourself one before whom you dare not trip, and till you have a bashfulness and respect for yourself, 'Obversentur species honestæ animo;'[43] present continually to your imagination Cato, Phocion, and Aristides, in whose presence the fools themselves will hide their faults, and make them controllers of all your intentions; should these deviate from virtue, your respect to those will set you right; they will keep you in the way to be contented with yourself; to borrow nothing of any other but yourself; to stay and fix your soul in certain and limited

---

[38] Epicurus and Seneca. See Seneca, Ep., 21, who cites a passage from the Letter of Epicurus to Idomeneus, differing from that given by Diogenes Laertius.

[39] Seneca, Ep., 7.

[40] Idem, Ep., 7, ascribes these words to Democritus.

[41] Idem, Ep., 68.

[42] Idem, Ep., 25.

[43] "Let just and honest things be ever present to the mind." — Cicero, Tusc. Quæs., ii. 22.

thoughts, wherein she may please herself, and having understood the true and real goods, which men the more enjoy the more they understand, to rest satisfied, without desire of prolongation of life or name." This is the precept of the true and natural philosophy, not of a boasting and prating philosophy, such as that of the two former.[44]

[44] Pliny the younger and Cicero.

Of the Inequality Amongst Us

PLUTARCH SAYS SOMEWHERE[1] that he does not find so great a difference betwixt beast and beast as he does betwixt man and man; which he says in reference to the internal qualities and perfections of the soul. And, in truth I find so vast a distance betwixt Epaminondas, according to my judgment of him, and some that I know, who are yet men of good sense, that I could willingly enhance upon Plutarch, and say that there is more difference betwixt such and such a man than there is betwixt such a man and such a beast:

> "Hem! vir viro quid præstat!"[2]

and that there are as many and innumerable degrees of minds as there are cubits betwixt this and heaven. But as touching the estimate of men, 'tis strange that, ourselves excepted, no other creature is esteemed beyond its proper qualities; we commend a horse for his strength and sureness of foot,

> "Volucrem
> Sic laudamus equum, facili cui plurima palma
> Fervet, et exsultat rauco victoria circo,"[3]

and not for his rich caparison; a greyhound for his speed of heels, not for his fine collar; a hawk for her wing, not for her gesses and bells. Why, in like manner, do we not value a man for what is properly his own? He has a great train, a beautiful palace, so much credit, so many thousand pounds a year: all these are about him, but not in him. You will not buy a pig in a poke: if you cheapen a horse[4] you will see him stripped of his

---

[1] In the essay, The Brute Creation Exercises Reason.

[2] "Ah! how much may one man surpass another!" — Terence, Eunuchus, ii. 3, 1.

[3] "So we praise the swift horse, for whom many an applauding hand glows, and victory exults among the hoarse shouts of the circus." — Juvenal, viii. 57.

[4] Seneca, Ep., 80.

housing-cloths, you will see him naked and open to your eye; or if he be
clothed, as they anciently were wont to present them to princes to sell,
'tis only on the less important parts, that you may not so much consider
the beauty of his colour or the breadth of his crupper, as principally to
examine his legs, eyes, and feet, which are the members of greatest use:

> "Regibus hic mos est: ubi equos mercantur, opertos
> Inspiciunt; ne, si facies, ut sæpe, decora
> Molli fulta pede est, emptorem inducat hiantem,
> Quod pulchræ clunes, breve quod caput, ardua cervix:"[5]

why, in giving your estimate of a man, do you prize him wrapped and
muffled up in clothes? He then discovers nothing to you but such parts
as are not in the least his own, and conceals those by which alone one
may rightly judge of his value. 'Tis the price of the blade that you inquire
into, not of the scabbard: you would not peradventure bid a farthing for
him, if you saw him stripped. You are to judge him by himself, and not
by what he wears; and, as one of the ancients very pleasantly said: "Do
you know why you repute him tall? You reckon withal the height of his
pattens."[6] The pedestal is no part of the statue. Measure him without his
stilts; let him lay aside his revenues and his titles, let him present himself
in his shirt. Then examine if his body be sound and sprightly, active and
disposed to perform its functions. What soul has he? Is she beautiful,
capable, and happily provided of all her faculties? Is she rich of what is
her own, or of what she has borrowed? Has fortune no hand in the affair?
Can she, without winking, stand the lightning of swords? is she indifferent whether her life expire by the mouth or through the throat? Is she
settled, even and content? This is what is to be examined, and by that
you are to judge of the vast differences betwixt man and man. Is he

> "Sapiens, sibique imperiosus,
> Quem neque pauperies, neque mors, neque vincula terrent;
> Responsare cupidinibus, contemnere honores
> Fortis; et in seipso totus teres atque rotundus,
> Externi ne quid valeat per læve morari;
> In quem manca ruit semper fortuna?"[7]

---

[5] "When kings and great folks buy horses, as 'tis the custom, in their housings, they take care
to inspect very closely, lest a short head, a high crest, a broad haunch, and ample chest stand
upon an old beaten hoof, to gull the buyer." — Horace, Sat., i. 2, 86.

[6] Seneca, Ep., 76.

[7] "The wise man, who has command over himself: whom neither poverty, nor death, nor
chains affright; who has the strength and courage to restrain his appetites and to contemn
honours; who has his all within himself; a mind well turned and even balanced, like a smooth
and perfect ball, which nothing external can stop in its course; whom fortune assails in
vain." — Horace, Sat., ii. 7, 83.

such a man is five hundred cubits above kingdoms and duchies; he is an absolute monarch in and to himself.

> "Sapiens, . . . Pol! ipse fingit fortunam sibi;"[8]

what remains for him to covet or desire?

> "Nonne videmus,
> Nil aliud sibi naturam latrare, nisi ut, quoi
> Corpore sejunctus dolor absit, mente fruatur,
> Jucundo sensu, cura semotu' metuque?"[9]

Compare with such a one the common rabble of mankind, stupid and mean-spirited, servile, instable, and continually floating with the tempest of various passions, that tosses and tumbles them to and fro, and all depending upon others, and you will find a greater distance than betwixt heaven and earth; and yet the blindness of common usage is such that we make little or no account of it; whereas, if we consider a peasant and a king, a nobleman and a vassal, a magistrate and a private man, a rich man and a poor, there appears a vast disparity, though they differ no more, as a man may say, than in their breeches.

In Thrace the king was distinguished from his people after a very pleasant and especial manner; he had a religion by himself, a god all his own, and which his subjects were not to presume to adore, which was Mercury, whilst, on the other hand, he disdained to have anything to do with theirs, Mars, Bacchus, and Diana. And yet they are no other than pictures that make no essential dissimilitude; for as you see actors in a play representing the person of a duke or an emperor upon the stage, and immediately after return to their true and original condition of valets and porters, so the emperor, whose pomp and lustre so dazzle you in public,

> "Scilicet et grandes viridi cum luce smaragdi
> Auro includuntur, teriturque thalassina vestis
> Assidue, et Veneris sudorem exercita potat;"[10]

do but peep behind the curtain, and you will see nothing more than an ordinary man, and peradventure more contemptible than the meanest of his subjects: "ille beatus introrsum est, istius bracteata felicitas est;"[11]

---

[8] "The wise man is the master of his own fortune." — Plautus, Trin., ii. 2, 84.

[9] "Do we not see that man's nature asks no more than that, free from bodily pain, he may exercise his mind agreeably, exempt from fear and anxiety?" — Lucretius, ii. 16.

[10] "Because he wears great emeralds richly set in gold, darting green lustre; and the sea-blue silken robe, worn with pressure, and moist with illicit love." — Lucretius, iv. 1123.

[11] "True happiness lies within, the other is but a counterfeit felicity." — Seneca, Ep., 115.

cowardice, irresolution, ambition, spite, and envy agitate him as much
as another.

> "Non enim gazæ, neque consularis,
> Summovet lictor miseros tumultus
> Mentis, et curas laqueata circum
> Tecta volantes."[12]

Care and fear attack him even in the centre of his battalions.

> "Re veraque metus hominum, curæque sequaces
> Nec metuunt sonitus armorum, nec fera tela;
> Audacterque inter reges, rerumque potentes
> Versantur, neque fulgorem reverentur ab auro."[13]

Do fevers, gout, and apoplexies spare him any more than one of us?
When old age hangs heavy upon his shoulders, can the yeomen of his
guard ease him of the burden? When he is astounded with the apprehension of death, can the gentlemen of his bedchamber comfort and
assure him? When jealousy or any other caprice swims in his brain, can
our compliments and ceremonies restore him to his good-humour? The
canopy embroidered with pearl and gold he lies under has no virtue
against a violent fit of the colic.

> "Nec calidæ citius decedunt corpore febres
> Textilibus si in picturis, ostroque rubenti
> Jactaris, quam si plebeia in veste cubandum est."[14]

The flatterers of Alexander the Great possessed him that he was the son
of Jupiter; but being one day wounded, and observing the blood stream
from his wound: "What say you now, my masters," said he, "is not this
blood of a crimson colour and purely human? This is not of the
complexion of that which Homer makes to issue from the wounded
gods."[15] The poet Hermodorus had written a poem in honour of Antigonus, wherein he called him the son of the sun: "He who has the
emptying of my close-stool," said Antigonus, "knows to the contrary."[16]

---

[12] "For not treasures, nor the consular lictor, can remove the miserable tumults of the mind,
nor cares that fly about gilded ceilings." — Horace, Od., ii. 16, 9.

[13] "The fears and pursuing cares of men fear not the clash of arms nor points of darts, and
mingle boldly with great kings and potentates, and respect not their purple and glittering
gold." — Lucretius, ii. 47.

[14] "Fevers quit a man no sooner because he is stretched on a couch of rich tapestry than if he
be in a coarse blanket." — Idem, ii. 34.

[15] Plutarch, Apothegms, art. Alexander.

[16] Idem, ibid., art. Antigonus.

He is but a man at best, and if he be deformed or ill qualified from his birth, the empire of the universe cannot set him to rights;

> "Puellæ
> Hunc rapiant; quidquid calcaverit hic, rosa fiat,"[17]

what of all that, if he be a fool? even pleasure and good fortune are not relished without vigour and understanding.

> "Hæc perinde sunt, ut illius animus, qui ea possidet:
> Qui uti scit, ei bona; illi, qui non utitur recte, mala."[18]

Whatever the benefits of fortune are, they yet require a palate fit to relish them. 'Tis fruition, and not possession, that renders us happy.

> "Non domus et fundus, non æris acervus, et auri,
> Ægroto domini deduxit corpore febres,
> Non animo curas. Valeat possessor oportet,
> Qui comportatis rebus bene cogitat uti:
> Qui cupit, aut metuit, juvat illum sic domus aut res,
> Ut lippum pictæ tabulæ, fomenta podagram."[19]

He is a sot, his taste is palled and flat; he no more enjoys what he has than one that has a cold relishes the flavour of canary, or than a horse is sensible of his rich caparison. Plato is in the right when he tells us that health, beauty, vigour, and riches, and all the other things called goods, are equally evil to the unjust as good to the just, and the evil on the contrary the same. And therefore where the body and the mind are in disorder, to what use serve these external conveniences: considering that the least prick with a pin, or the least passion of the soul, is sufficient to deprive one of the pleasure of being sole monarch of the world. At the first twitch of the gout it signifies much to be called Sir and Your Majesty,

> "Totus et argento conflatus, totus et auro;"[20]

---

[17] "What though girls carry him off; though, wherever he steps, there spring up a rose?" — Persius, Sat., ii. 38.

[18] "Things are, as are the souls of their possessors; good, if well used; ill, if abused." — Terence, Heaut., i. 3, 21.

[19] "'Tis not lands, or heaps of gold and silver, that can banish fevers from the body of the sick owner, or cares from his mind. The possessor must be sound and healthy, if he would have the true realisation of his wealth. To him who is covetous, or timorous, his house and land are as a picture to a blind man, or a fomentation to a gouty man." — Horace, Ep., i. 2, 47.

[20] "A mass of gold and silver." — Tibullus, i. 2, 70.

does he not forget his palaces and grandeurs? If he be angry, can his being a prince keep him from looking red and looking pale, and grinding his teeth like a madman? Now, if he be a man of parts and of right nature, royalty adds very little to his happiness;

> "Si ventri bene, si lateri est, pedibusque tuis, nil
> Divitiæ poterunt regales addere majus;"[21]

he discerns 'tis nothing but counterfeit and gullery. Nay, perhaps he would be of King Seleucus' opinion, that he who knew the weight of a sceptre would not stoop to pick it up, if he saw it lying before him, so great and painful are the duties incumbent upon a good king.[22] Assuredly it can be no easy task to rule others, when we find it so hard a matter to govern ourselves; and as to dominion, that seems so charming, the frailty of human judgment and the difficulty of choice in things that are new and doubtful considered, I am very much of opinion that it is far more easy and pleasant to follow than to lead; and that it is a great settlement and satisfaction of mind to have only one path to walk in, and to have none to answer for but a man's self;

> "Ut satius multo jam sit parere quietum.
> Quam regere imperio res velle."[23]

To which we may add that saying of Cyrus, that no man was fit to rule but he who in his own worth was of greater value than those he was to govern; but King Hiero in Xenophon says further, that in the fruition even of pleasure itself they are in a worse condition than private men; forasmuch as the opportunities and facility they have of commanding those things at will takes off from the delight that ordinary folks enjoy.

> "Pinguis amor, nimiumque patens, in tædia nobis
> Vertitur, et, stomacho dulcis ut esca, nocet."[24]

Can we think that the singing boys of the choir take any great delight in music? the satiety rather renders it troublesome and tedious to them. Feasts, balls, masquerades and tiltings delight such as but rarely see, and desire to see, them; but having been frequently at such entertainments, the relish of them grows flat and insipid. Nor do women so much delight those who make a common practice of the sport. He who will not give

---

[21] "If your stomach is sound, your lungs and feet in good order, you need no regal riches to make you happy." — Horace, Ep., i. 12, 5.

[22] Plutarch, If a Sage Should Meddle with Affairs of State, c. 12.

[23] "'Tis much better calmly to obey than wish to rule." — Lucretius, v. 1126.

[24] "Love that is listless and too facile becomes wearisome, as insipid meats are nauseous to the stomach." — Ovid, Amor., ii. 19, 25.

himself leisure to be thirsty can never find the true pleasure of drinking. Farces and tumbling tricks are pleasant to the spectators, but a wearisome toil to those by whom they are performed. And that this is so, we see that princes divert themselves sometimes in disguising their quality, awhile to depose themselves, and to stoop to the poor and ordinary way of living of the meanest of their people.

> "Plerumque gratæ principibus vices,
> Mundæque parvo sub lare pauperum
> Cœnæ, sine aulæis et ostro,
> Sollicitam explicuere frontem."[25]

Nothing is so distasteful and clogging as abundance. What appetite would not be baffled to see three hundred women at its mercy, as the grand signor has in his seraglio? And, of his ancestors, what fruition or taste of sport did he reserve to himself, who never went hawking without seven thousand falconers? And besides all this, I fancy that this lustre of grandeur brings with it no little disturbance and uneasiness upon the enjoyment of the most tempting pleasures; the great are too conspicuous and lie too open to every one's view. Neither do I know to what end a man should more require of them to conceal their errors, since what is only reputed indiscretion in us, the people in them brand with the names of tyranny and contempt of the laws, and, besides their proclivity to vice, are apt to hold that it is a heightening of pleasure to them, to insult over and to trample upon public observances. Plato, indeed, in his "Gorgias," defines a tyrant to be one who in a city has licence to do whatever his own will leads him to do; and by reason of this impunity, the display and publication of their vices do ofttimes more mischief than the vice itself. Every one fears to be pried into and overlooked; but princes are so, even to their very gestures, looks and thoughts, the people conceiving they have right and title to be judges of them: besides that the blemishes of the great naturally appear greater by reason of the eminence and lustre of the place where they are seated, and that a mole or a wart appears greater in them than a wide gash in others. And this is the reason why the poets feign the amours of Jupiter to be performed in the disguises of so many borrowed shapes, and that amongst the many amorous practices they lay to his charge, there is only one, as I remember, where he appears in his own majesty and grandeur.

But let us return to Hiero, who further complains of the inconveniences he found in his royalty, in that he could not look abroad and travel the world at liberty, being as it were a prisoner in the bounds and

---

[25] "The rich and great are often pleased with variety; and a plain supper in a poor cottage, where there are neither tapestry nor beds of purple, has made their anxious brow smooth." — Horace, Od., iii. 29, 13, which has *divitibus*, not *principibus*.

limits of his own dominion, and that in all his actions he was evermore surrounded with an importunate crowd. And in truth, to see our kings sit all alone at table, environed with so many people prating about them, and so many strangers staring upon them, as they always are, I have often been moved rather to pity than to envy their condition. King Alfonso was wont to say, that in this, asses were in a better condition than kings, their masters permitting them to feed at their own ease and pleasure, a favour that kings cannot obtain of their servants. And it has never come into my fancy that it could be of any great benefit to the life of a man of sense to have twenty people prating about him when he is at stool; or that the services of a man of ten thousand livres a year, or that has taken Casale or defended Siena, should be either more commodious or more acceptable to him, than those of a good groom of the chamber who understands his place. The advantages of sovereignty are in a manner but imaginary: every degree of fortune has in it some image of principality. Cæsar calls all the lords of France, having free franchise within their own demesnes, roitelets or petty kings; and in truth, the name of sire excepted, they go pretty far towards kingship; for do but look into the provinces remote from court, as Brittany for example, take notice of the train, the vassals, the officers, the employments, service, ceremony, and state of a lord who lives retired from court in his own house, amongst his own tenants and servants; and observe withal, the flight of his imagination, there is nothing more royal; he hears talk of his master once a year, as of a king of Persia, without taking any further recognition of him, than by some remote kindred his secretary keeps in some musty record. And, to speak the truth, our laws are easy enough, so easy that a gentleman of France scarce feels the weight of sovereignty pinch his shoulders above twice in his life. Real and effectual subjection only concerns such amongst us as voluntarily thrust their necks under the yoke, and who design to get wealth and honours by such services: for a man that loves his own fireside, and can govern his house without falling by the ears with his neighbours or engaging in suits of law, is as free as a duke of Venice. "Paucos servitus, plures servitutem tenent."[26]

But that which Hiero is most concerned at is, that he finds himself stripped of all friendship, deprived of all mutual society, wherein the true and most perfect fruition of human life consists. For what testimony of affection and goodwill can I extract from him that owes me, whether he will or no, all that he is able to do? Can I form any assurance of his real respect to me, from his humble way of speaking and submissive behaviour, when these are ceremonies it is not in his choice to deny? The honour we receive from those that fear us, is not honour; those respects are paid to royalty and not to me.

---

[26] "Servitude enchains few, but many enchain themselves to servitude." — Seneca, Ep., 22.

"Maximum hoc regni bonum est,
Quod facta domini cogitur populus sui
Quam ferre, tam laudare."[27]

Do I not see that the wicked and the good king, he that is hated and he that is beloved, have the one as much reverence paid him as the other? My predecessor was, and my successor shall be, served with the same ceremony and state. If my subjects do me no harm, 'tis no evidence of any good affection; why should I look upon it as such, seeing it is not in their power to do it if they would? No one follows me or obeys my commands, upon the account of any friendship betwixt him and me; there can be no contracting of friendship, where there is so little relation and correspondence: my own height has put me out of the familiarity of and intelligence with men: there is too great disparity and disproportion betwixt us. They follow me either upon the account of decency and custom; or rather my fortune, than me, to increase their own. All they say to me, or do for me, is but outward paint, appearance, their liberty being on all parts restrained by the great power and authority I have over them. I see nothing about me but what is dissembled and disguised.

The Emperor Julian being one day applauded by his courtiers for his exact justice: "I should be proud of these praises," said he, "did they come from persons that durst condemn or disapprove the contrary, in case I should do it."[28] All the real advantages of princes are common to them with men of meaner condition ('tis for the gods to mount winged horses and feed upon ambrosia): they have no other sleep, nor other appetite than we; the steel they arm themselves withal, is of no better temper than that we also use; their crowns neither defend them from the rain nor the sun.

Diocletian, who wore a crown so fortunate and revered, resigned it to retire to the felicity of a private life; and some time after, the necessity of public affairs requiring that he should reassume his charge, he made answer to those who came to court him to it: "You would not offer," said he, "to persuade me to this had you seen the fine order of the trees I have planted in my orchard, and the fair melons I have sown in my garden."[29]

In Anacharsis' opinion, the happiest state of government would be where, all other things being equal, precedency should be measured out by the virtues, and repulses by the vices of men.[30]

---

[27] "'Tis the greatest benefits of kings, that their subjects are bound, whatever they say or do, not only to submit, but also to praise it." — Idem, Thyestes, ii. 1, 30.

[28] Ammianus Marcellinus, xxii. 10.

[29] Aurelius Victor, art. Diocletian.

[30] Plutarch, Banquet of the Seven Sages, c. 13.

When King Pyrrhus prepared for his expedition into Italy, his wise counsellor Cyneas, to make him sensible of the vanity of his ambition: "Well, sir," said he, "to what end do you make all this mighty preparation?" "To make myself master of Italy," replied the king. "And what after that is done?" said Cyneas. "I will pass over into Gaul and Spain," said the other. "And what then?" "I will then go to subdue Africa; and lastly, when I have brought the whole world to my subjection, I will sit down and rest content at my own ease." "For God sake, sir," replied Cyneas, "tell me what hinders that you may not, if you please, be now in the condition you speak of? Why do you not now at this instant, settle yourself in the state you seem to aim at, and spare all the labour and hazard you interpose?"[31]

> "Nimirum, quia non bene norat, quæ esset habendi
> Finis, et omnino quoad crescat vera voluptas."[32]

I will conclude with an old versicle, that I think very apt to the purpose. "Mores cuique sui fingunt fortunam."[33]

---

[31] Idem, Pyrrhus, c. 7.

[32] "Truly because they do not know what is the proper limit of acquisition, and how far real pleasure extends." — Lucretius, v. 1431. The text has *quia non cognovit*.

[33] "Every man frames his own fortune." — Cornelius Nepos, Life of Atticus, c. ii.

Of Books

I MAKE NO doubt but that I often happen to speak of things that are much better and more truly handled by those who are masters of the trade. You have here purely an essay of my natural parts, and not of those acquired: and whoever shall catch me tripping in ignorance, will not in any sort get the better of me; for I should be very unwilling to become responsible to another for my writings, who am not so to myself, nor satisfied with them. Whoever goes in quest of knowledge, let him fish for it where it is to be found; there is nothing I so little profess. These are fancies of my own, by which I do not pretend to discover things but to lay open myself; they may, peradventure, one day be known to me, or have formerly been, according as fortune has been able to bring me in place where they have been explained; but I have utterly forgotten it; and if I am a man of some reading, I am a man of no retention; so that I can promise no certainty, more than to make known to what point the knowledge I now have has risen. Therefore, let none lay stress upon the matter I write, but upon my method in writing it. Let them observe, in what I borrow, if I have known how to choose what is proper to raise or help the invention, which is always my own. For I make others say for me, not before but after me, what, either for want of language or want of sense, I cannot myself so well express. I do not number my borrowings, I weigh them; and had I designed to raise their value by number, I had made them twice as many; they are all, or within a very few, so famed and ancient authors, that they seem, methinks, themselves sufficiently to tell who they are, without giving me the trouble. In reasons, comparisons, and arguments, if I transplant any into my own soil, and confound them amongst my own, I purposely conceal the author, to awe the temerity of those precipitate censors who fall upon all sorts of writings, particularly the late ones, of men yet living, and in the vulgar tongue which puts every one into a capacity of criticizing and which seem to convict the conception and design as vulgar also. I will have them give Plutarch a fillip on my nose, and rail against Seneca when they think

they rail at me. I must shelter my own weakness under these great
reputations. I shall love any one that can unplume me, that is, by
clearness of understanding and judgment, and by the sole distinction
of the force and beauty of the discourse. For I who, for want of
memory, am at every turn at a loss to pick them out of their national
livery, am yet wise enough to know, by the measure of my own
abilities, that my soil is incapable of producing any of those rich
flowers that I there find growing; and that all the fruits of my own
growth are not worth any one of them. For this, indeed, I hold myself
responsible; if I get in my own way; if there be any vanity and defect in
my writings which I do not of myself perceive nor can discern, when
pointed out to me by another; for many faults escape our eye, but the
infirmity of judgment consists in not being able to discern them when,
by another laid open to us. Knowledge and truth may be in us without
judgment, and judgment also without them; but the confession of
ignorance is one of the finest and surest testimonies of judgment that I
know. I have no other officer to put my writings in rank and file, but
only fortune. As things come into my head, I heap them one upon
another; sometimes they advance in whole bodies, sometimes in single
file. I would that every one should see my natural and ordinary pace,
irregular as it is; I suffer myself to jog on at my own rate. Neither are
these subjects which a man is not permitted to be ignorant in, or
casually and at a venture, to discourse of. I could wish to have a more
perfect knowledge of things, but I will not buy it so dear as it costs. My
design is to pass over easily, and not laboriously, the remainder of my
life; there is nothing that I will cudgel my brains about; no, not even
knowledge, of what value soever.

I seek, in the reading of books, only to please myself, by an honest
diversion; or, if I study, 'tis for no other science than what treats of
the knowledge of myself, and instructs me how to die and how to live
well.

"Has meus ad metas sudet oportet equus."[1]

I do not bite my nails about the difficulties I meet with in my reading; after a charge or two, I give them over. Should I insist upon them,
I should both lose myself and time; for I have an impatient understanding, that must be satisfied at first: what I do not discern at
once, is by persistence rendered more obscure. I do nothing without
gaiety; continuation and a too obstinate endeavour, darkens, stupefies,
and tires my judgment. My sight is confounded and dissipated with
poring; I must withdraw it, and refer my discovery to new attempts; just

---

[1] "My horse must be trained to this course." — Propertius, iv. 1, 70.

as to judge rightly of the lustre of scarlet, we are taught to pass the eye lightly over it, and again to run it over at several sudden and reiterated glances. If one book do not please me, I take another; and never meddle with any, but at such times as I am weary of doing nothing. I care not much for new ones, because the old seem fuller and stronger; neither do I converse much with Greek authors, because my judgment cannot do its work with imperfect intelligence of the material.[2]

Amongst books that are simply pleasant, of the moderns, Boccaccio's Decameron, Rabelais, and the Basia of Johannes Secundus (if those may be ranged under the title) are worth reading for amusement. As to Amadis, and such kind of stuff, they had not credit to take me, so much as in my childhood. And I will, moreover, say, whether boldly or rashly, that this old, heavy soul of mine is now no longer tickled with Ariosto, no, nor with Ovid; his facility and inventions, with which I was formerly so ravished, are now of no more relish, and I can hardly have the patience to read them. I speak my opinion freely of all things, even of those that, perhaps, exceed my capacity, and that I do not conceive to be, in any wise, under my jurisdiction. And, accordingly, the judgment I deliver, is to show the measure of my own sight, and not of the things I make so bold to criticise. When I find myself disgusted with Plato's "Axiochus,"[3] as with a work, with due respect to such an author be it spoken, without force, my judgment does not believe itself: it is not so arrogant as to oppose the authority of so many other famous judgments of antiquity, which it considers as its tutors and masters, and with whom it is rather content to err; in such a case, it condemns itself either to stop at the outward bark, not being able to penetrate to the heart, or to consider it by some false light. It is content with only securing itself from trouble and disorder; as to its own weakness, it frankly acknowledges and confesses it. It thinks it gives a just interpretation to the appearances by its conceptions presented to it; but they are weak and imperfect. Most of the fables of Æsop have diverse senses and meanings, of which the mythologists chose some one that quadrates well to the fable; but, for the most part, 'tis but the first face that presents itself and is superficial only; there yet remain others more vivid, essential, and profound, into which they have not been able to penetrate; and just so 'tis with me.

But, to pursue the business of this essay, I have always thought that, in poesy, Virgil, Lucretius, Catullus, and Horace by many degrees excel the rest; and signally, Virgil in his Georgics, which I look upon as

---

[2] Montaigne refers to his imperfect knowledge of the Greek language.

[3] The "Axiochus" is not by Plato, as Diogenes Laertius admitted. It is attributed by some to Æschines the Socratic, and by others to Xenocrates of Chalcedon. — Le Clerc.

the most accomplished piece in poetry; and in comparison of which a man may easily discern that there are some places in his Æneids, to which the author would have given a little more of the file, had he had leisure: and the fifth book of his Æneids seems to me the most perfect. I also love Lucan, and willingly read him, not so much for his style, as for his own worth, and the truth and solidity of his opinions and judgments. As for Terence, that model of the refined elegancies and grace of the Latin tongue, I find him admirable in his vivid representation of our manners and the movements of the soul; our actions throw me at every turn, upon him; and I cannot read him so often that I do not still discover some new grace and beauty. Such as lived near Virgil's time were scandalised that some should compare him with Lucretius. I am, I confess, of opinion that the comparison is, in truth, very unequal; a belief that, nevertheless, I have much ado to assure myself in, when I come upon some excellent passage in Lucretius. But if they were so angry at this comparison, what would they say to the brutish and barbarous stupidity of those who, nowadays, compare him with Ariosto? Would not Ariosto himself say?

"O seclum insipiens et inficetum!"[4]

I think the ancients had more reason to be angry with those who compared Plautus with Terence, though much nearer the mark, than Lucretius with Virgil. It makes much for the estimation and preference of Terence, that the father of Roman eloquence has him so often, and alone of his class, in his mouth; and the opinion that the best judge of Roman poets[5] has passed upon his companion. I have often observed that those of our times, who take upon them to write comedies (in imitation of the Italians, who are happy enough in that way of writing), take three or four plots of those of Plautus or Terence to make one of their own, and crowd five or six of Boccaccio's novels into one single comedy. That which makes them so load themselves with matter is the diffidence they have of being able to support themselves with their own strength. They must find out something to lean to; and not having of their own stuff wherewith to entertain us, they bring in the story to supply the defect of language. It is quite otherwise with my author; the elegance and perfection of his way of speaking makes us lose the appetite of his plot; his refined grace and elegance of diction everywhere occupy us: he is so pleasant throughout,

"Liquidus, puroque simillimus amni,"[6]

---

[4] "O stupid and tasteless age." — Catullus, xliii. 8.

[5] Horace, de Art. Poetica, 279.

[6] "Liquid, and like a crystal stream." — Horace, Ep., ii. 2, 120.

and so possesses the soul with his graces that we forget those of his fable. This same consideration carries me further: I observe that the best of the ancient poets have avoided affectation and the hunting after, not only fantastic Spanish and Petrarchal elevations, but even the softer and more gentle touches, which are the ornament of all succeeding poesy. And yet there is no good judgment that will condemn this in the ancients, and that does not incomparably more admire the equal polish, and that perpetual sweetness and flourishing beauty of Catullus's epigrams, than all the stings with which Martial arms the tails of his. This is by the same reason that I gave before, and as Martial says of himself: "Minus illi ingenio laborandum fuit, in cujus locum materia successerat."[7] The first, without being moved, or without getting angry, make themselves sufficiently felt; they have matter enough of laughter throughout, they need not tickle themselves; the others have need of foreign assistance; as they have the less wit they must have the more body; they mount on horseback, because they are not able to stand on their own legs. As in our balls, those mean fellows who teach to dance, not being able to represent the presence and dignity of our noblesse, are fain to put themselves forward with dangerous jumping, and other strange motions and tumblers' tricks; and the ladies are less put to it in dances, where there are various coupees, changes, and quick motions of body, than in some other of a more sedate kind, where they are only to move a natural pace, and to represent their ordinary grace and presence. And so I have seen good drolls, when in their own everyday clothes, and with the same face they always wear, give us all the pleasure of their art, when their apprentices, not yet arrived at such a pitch of perfection, are fain to meal their faces, put themselves into ridiculous disguises, and make a hundred grotesque faces to give us whereat to laugh. This conception of mine is nowhere more demonstrable than in comparing the Æneid with Orlando Furioso; of which we see the first, by dint of wing, flying in a brave and lofty place, and always following his point; the latter, fluttering and hopping from tale to tale, as from branch to branch, not daring to trust his wings but in very short flights, and perching at every turn, lest his breath and strength should fail;

"Excursusque breves tentat."[8]

These, then, as to this sort of subjects, are the authors that best please me.

---

[7] "He had all the less for his wit to do that the subject itself supplied what was necessary." — Martial, præf. ad lib. viii.

[8] "Making short runs." — Virgil, Georgics, iv. 194.

As to what concerns my other reading, that mixes a little more profit
with the pleasure, and whence I learn how to marshal my opinions
and conditions, the books that serve me to this purpose are Plutarch,
since he has been translated into French, and Seneca. Both of these
have this notable convenience suited to my humour, that the knowledge I there seek is discoursed in loose pieces, that do not require from
me any trouble of reading long, of which I am incapable. Such are the
minor works of the first and the epistles of the latter, which are the best
and most profiting of all their writings. 'Tis no great attempt to take
one of them in hand, and I give over at pleasure; for they have no
sequence or dependence upon one another. These authors, for the
most part, concur in useful and true opinions; and there is this parallel
betwixt them, that fortune brought them into the world about the same
century: they were both tutors to two Roman emperors: both sought
out from foreign countries: both rich and both great men. Their
instruction is the cream of philosophy, and delivered after a plain and
pertinent manner. Plutarch is more uniform and constant; Seneca
more various and waving: the last toiled and bent his whole strength to
fortify virtue against weakness, fear, and vicious appetites; the other
seems more to slight their power, and to disdain to alter his pace and to
stand upon his guard. Plutarch's opinions are Platonic, gentle, and
accommodated to civil society; those of the other are Stoical and
Epicurean, more remote from the common use, but, in my opinion,
more individually commodious and more firm. Seneca seems to lean a
little to the tyranny of the emperors of his time, and only seems; for I
take it for certain that he speaks against his judgment when he condemns the action of the generous murderers of Cæsar. Plutarch is
frank throughout: Seneca abounds with brisk touches and sallies;
Plutarch with things that heat and move you more; this contents and
pays you better: he guides us, the other pushes us on.

As to Cicero, those of his works that are most useful to my design are
they that treat of philosophy, especially moral. But boldly to confess
the truth (for since one has passed the barriers of impudence, off with
the bridle), his way of writing, and that of all other long-winded
authors, appears to me very tedious: for his prefaces, definitions, divi-
sions, and etymologies take up the greatest part of his work: whatever
there is of life and marrow is smothered and lost in the long preparation. When I have spent an hour in reading him, which is a great deal
for me, and try to recollect what I have thence extracted of juice and
substance, for the most part I find nothing but wind; for he is not yet
come to the arguments that serve to his purpose, and to the reasons
that properly help to form the knot I seek. For me, who only desire to
become more wise, not more learned or eloquent, these logical and
Aristotelian dispositions of parts are of no use. I would have a man

begin with the main proposition. I know well enough what death and pleasure are; let no man give himself the trouble to anatomise them to me. I look for good and solid reasons, at the first dash, to instruct me how to stand their shock, for which purpose neither grammatical subtleties nor the quaint contexture of words and argumentations are of any use at all. I am for discourses that give the first charge into the heart of the redoubt; his languish about the subject; they are proper for the schools, for the bar, and for the pulpit, where we have leisure to nod, and may awake, a quarter of an hour after, time enough to find again the thread of the discourse. It is necessary to speak after this manner to judges, whom a man has a design to gain over, right or wrong, to children and common people, to whom a man must say all, and see what will come of it. I would not have an author make it his business to render me attentive: or that he should cry out fifty times *Oyez*,[9] as the heralds do. The Romans, in their religious exercises, began with *Hoc age:*[10] as we in ours do with *Sursum corda;*[11] these are so many words lost to me: I come already fully prepared from my chamber. I need no allurement, no invitation, no sauce; I eat the meat raw, so that, instead of whetting my appetite by these preparatives, they tire and pall it. Will the licence of the time excuse my sacrilegious boldness if I censure the dialogism of Plato himself as also dull and heavy, too much stifling the matter, and lament so much time lost by a man, who had so many better things to say, in so many long and needless preliminary interlocutions? My ignorance will better excuse me in that I understand not Greek so well as to discern the beauty of his language. I generally choose books that use sciences, not such as only lead to them. The two first, and Pliny, and their like, have nothing of this *Hoc age*; they will have to do with men already instructed; or if they have, 'tis a substantial *Hoc age*, and that has a body by itself. I also delight in reading the Epistles to Atticus, not only because they contain a great deal of the history and affairs of his time, but much more because I therein discover much of his own private humours; for I have a singular curiosity, as I have said elsewhere, to pry into the souls and the natural and true opinions of the authors with whom I converse. A man may indeed judge of their parts, but not of their manners nor of themselves, by the writings they exhibit upon the theatre of the world. I have a thousand times lamented the loss of the treatise Brutus wrote upon virtue, for it is well to learn the theory from those who best know the practice. But seeing the matter preached and the preacher

---

[9] ["Hear ye!"]

[10] ["This do."]

[11] ["Lift up your hearts."]

are different things, I would as willingly see Brutus in Plutarch, as in a book of his own. I would rather choose to be certainly informed of the conference he had in his tent with some particular friends of his the night before a battle, than of the harangue he made the next day to his army; and of what he did in his closet and his chamber, than what he did in the public square and in the senate. As to Cicero, I am of the common opinion that, learning excepted, he had no great natural excellence. He was a good citizen, of an affable nature, as all fat, heavy men, such as he was, usually are; but given to ease, and had, in truth, a mighty share of vanity and ambition. Neither do I know how to excuse him for thinking his poetry fit to be published; 'tis no great imperfection to make ill verses, but it is an imperfection not to be able to judge how unworthy his verses were of the glory of his name. For what concerns his eloquence, that is totally out of all comparison, and I believe it will never be equalled. The younger Cicero, who resembled his father in nothing but in name, whilst commanding in Asia, had several strangers one day at his table, and, amongst the rest, Cestius seated at the lower end, as men often intrude to the open tables of the great. Cicero asked one of his people who that man was, who presently told him his name; but he, as one who had his thoughts taken up with something else, and who had forgotten the answer made him, asking three or four times, over and over again, the same question, the fellow, to deliver himself from so many answers and to make him know him by some particular circumstance; "'tis that Cestius," said he, "of whom it was told you, that he makes no great account of your father's eloquence in comparison of his own." At which Cicero, being sud-denly nettled, commanded poor Cestius presently to be seized, and caused him to be very well whipped in his own presence;[12] a very discourteous entertainer! Yet even amongst those, who, all things con-sidered, have reputed his eloquence incomparable, there have been some, who have not stuck to observe some faults in it: as that great Brutus his friend, for example, who said 'twas a broken and feeble eloquence, *fractam et elumbem*.[13] The orators also, nearest to the age wherein he lived, reprehended in him the care he had of a certain long cadence in his periods, and particularly took notice of these words, *esse videatur*,[14] which he there so often makes use of. For my part, I more approve of a shorter style, and that comes more roundly off. He does, though, sometimes shuffle his parts more briskly together, but 'tis very seldom. I have myself taken notice of this one passage:

---

[12] Seneca, Suasor, 8.

[13] Tacitus, De Oratoribus, c. 18.

[14] ["It seems to be."] Idem, ibid., c. 23.

"Ego vero me minus diu senem mallem, quam esse senem antequam essem."[15]

The historians are my right ball, for they are pleasant and easy, and where man, in general, the knowledge of whom I hunt after, appears more vividly and entire than anywhere else:[16] the variety and truth of his internal qualities, in gross and piecemeal, the diversity of means by which he is united and knit, and the accidents that threaten him. Now those that write lives, by reason they insist more upon counsels than events, more upon what sallies from within, than upon what happens without, are the most proper for my reading; and, therefore, above all others, Plutarch is the man for me. I am very sorry we have not a dozen Laertii,[17] or that he was not further extended; for I am equally curious to know the lives and fortunes of these great instructors of the world, as to know the diversities of their doctrines and opinions. In this kind of study of histories, a man must tumble over, without distinction, all sorts of authors, old and new, French or foreign, there to know the things of which they variously treat. But Cæsar, in my opinion, particularly deserves to be studied, not for the knowledge of the history only, but for himself, so great an excellence and perfection he has above all the rest, though Sallust be one of the number. In earnest, I read this author with more reverence and respect than is usually allowed to human writings; one while considering him in his person, by his actions and miraculous greatness, and another in the purity and inimitable polish of his language, wherein he not only excels all other historians, as Cicero confesses,[18] but, peradventure, even Cicero himself; speaking of his enemies with so much sincerity in his judgment, that, the false colours with which he strives to palliate his evil cause, and the ordure of his pestilent ambition excepted, I think there is no fault to be objected against him, saving this, that he speaks too sparingly of himself, seeing so many great things could not have been performed under his conduct, but that his own personal acts must necessarily have had a greater share in them than he attributes to them.

I love historians, whether of the simple sort, or of the higher order. The simple, who have nothing of their own to mix with it, and who only make it their business to collect all that comes to their knowledge, and faithfully to record all things, without choice or discrimination, leave to us the entire judgment of discerning the truth. Such, for example

---

[15] "I had rather be old a brief time, than be old before old age." — Cicero, De Senect., c. 10.

[16] *i.e.*, The easiest of my amusements, the right ball, at tennis, being that which coming to the player from the right hand, is much easier played with. — Coste.

[17] Diogenes Laertius, who wrote the lives of the philosophers.

[18] Cicero, Brutus, c. 75.

amongst others, is honest Froissart, who has proceeded in his undertaking with so frank a plainness that, having committed an error, he is not ashamed to confess, and correct it in the place where the finger has been laid, and who represents to us even the variety of rumours that were then spread abroad, and the different reports that were made to him; 'tis the naked and inform matter of history, and of which every one may make his profit, according to his understanding. The more excellent sort of historians have judgment to pick out what is most worthy to be known; and, of two reports, to examine which is the most likely to be true: from the condition of princes and their humours, they conclude their counsels, and attribute to them words proper for the occasion; such have title to assume the authority of regulating our belief to what they themselves believe; but certainly, this privilege belongs to very few. For the middle sort of historians, of which the most part are, they spoil all; they will chew our meat for us; they take upon them to judge of, and consequently, to incline the history to their own fancy; for if the judgment lean to one side, a man cannot avoid wresting and writhing his narrative to that bias; they undertake to select things worthy to be known, and yet often conceal from us such a word, such a private action, as would much better instruct us; omit, as incredible, such things as they do not understand, and peradventure some, because they cannot express them well in good French or Latin. Let them display their eloquence and intelligence, and judge according to their own fancy: but let them, withal, leave us something to judge of after them, and neither alter nor disguise, by their abridgments and at their own choice, anything of the substance of the matter, but deliver it to us pure and entire in all its dimensions.

For the most part, and especially in these latter ages, persons are culled out for this work from amongst the common people, upon the sole consideration of well-speaking, as if we were to learn grammar from them; and the men so chosen have fair reason, being hired for no other end and pretending to nothing but babble, not to be very solicitous of any part but that, and so, with a fine gingle of words, prepare us a pretty contexture of reports they pick up in the streets. The only good histories are those that have been written by the persons themselves who held command in the affairs whereof they write, or who participated in the conduct of them, or, at least, who have had the conduct of others of the same nature. Such are almost all the Greek and Roman histories: for, several eye-witnesses having written of the same subject, in the time when grandeur and learning commonly met in the same person, if there happen to be an error, it must of necessity be a very slight one, and upon a very doubtful incident. What can a man expect from a physician who writes of war, or from a mere scholar, treating of the designs of princes? If we could take notice how scrupulous the Romans were in this, there would need but this example: Asinius Pollio found in the histories of

Cæsar himself, something misreported, a mistake occasioned, either by reason he could not have his eye in all parts of his army at once and had given credit to some individual persons who had not delivered him a very true account; or else, for not having had too perfect notice given him by his lieutenants of what they had done in his absence.[19] By which we may see, whether the inquisition after truth be not very delicate, when a man cannot believe the report of a battle from the knowledge of him who there commanded, nor from the soldiers who were engaged in it, unless, after the method of a judicial inquiry, the witnesses be confronted and objections considered upon the proof of the least detail of every incident. In good earnest the knowledge we have of our own affairs, is much more obscure: but that has been sufficiently handled by Bodin, and according to my own sentiment.[20] A little to aid the weakness of my memory (so extreme that it has happened to me more than once, to take books again into my hand as new and unseen, that I had carefully read over a few years before, and scribbled with my notes) I have adopted a custom of late, to note at the end of every book (that is, of those I never intend to read again) the time when I made an end on't, and the judgment I had made of it, to the end that this might, at least, represent to me the character and general idea I had conceived of the author in reading it; and I will here transcribe some of those annotations. I wrote this, some ten years ago, in my Guicciardini (of what language soever my books speak to me in, I always speak to them in my own): "He is a diligent historiographer, from whom, in my opinion, a man may learn the truth of the affairs of his time, as exactly as from any other; in the most of which he was himself also a personal actor, and in honourable command. There is no appearance that he disguised anything, either upon the account of hatred, favour, or vanity; of which the free censures he passes upon the great ones, and particularly, those by whom he was advanced and employed in commands of great trust and honour, as Pope Clement VII., give ample testimony. As to that part which he thinks himself the best at, namely, his digressions and discourses, he has indeed some very good, and enriched with fine features; but he is too fond of them: for, to leave nothing unsaid, having a subject so full, ample, almost infinite, he degenerates into pedantry and smacks a little of scholastic prattle. I have also observed this in him, that of so many souls and so many effects, so many motives and so many counsels as he judges, he never attributes any one to virtue, religion, or conscience, as if all these were utterly extinct in the world: and of all the actions, how brave

---

[19] Suetonius, Life of Cæsar, c. 56.

[20] In the work, by Jean Bodin, entitled "Methodus ad facilem historiarum cognitionem ["Method for the Ready Knowledge of History"]." 1566.

soever in outward show they appear in themselves, he always refers the cause and motive to some vicious occasion or some prospect of profit. It is impossible to imagine but that, amongst such an infinite number of actions as he makes mention of, there must be some one produced by the way of honest reason. No corruption could so universally have infected men that some one would not escape the contagion: which makes me suspect, that his own taste was vicious, whence it might happen that he judged other men by himself."

In my Philip de Comines, there is this written: "You will here find the language sweet and delightful, of a natural simplicity, the narration pure, with the good faith of the author conspicuous therein; free from vanity, when speaking of himself, and from affection or envy, when speaking of others: his discourses and exhortations rather accompanied with zeal and truth, than with any exquisite sufficiency; and, through-out, authority and gravity, which bespeak him a man of good extraction, and brought up in great affairs."

Upon the Memoirs of Monsieur du Bellay I find this: " 'Tis always pleasant to read things written by those that have experienced how they ought to be carried on; but withal, it cannot be denied but there is a manifest decadence in these two lords[21] from the freedom and liberty of writing that shine in the elder historians, such as the Sire de Joinville, the familiar companion of St. Louis; Eginhard, chancellor to Charle-magne; and of later date, Philip de Comines. What we have here is rather an apology for King Francis, against the Emperor Charles V., than history. I will not believe that they have falsified anything, as to matter of fact; but they make a common practice of twisting the judg-ment of events, very often contrary to reason, to our advantage, and of omitting whatsoever is ticklish to be handled in the life of their master; witness the proceedings of Messieurs de Montmorency and de Biron, which are here omitted: nay, so much as the very name of Madame d'Estampes is not here to be found. Secret actions an historian may conceal; but to pass over in silence what all the world knows and things that have drawn after them public and such high consequences, is an inexcusable defect. In fine, whoever has a mind to have a perfect knowledge of King Francis and the events of his reign, let him seek it elsewhere, if my advice may prevail. The only profit a man can reap from these Memoirs is in the special narrative of battles and other exploits of war wherein these gentlemen were personally engaged; in some words and private actions of the princes of their time, and in the treaties and negotiations carried on by the Seigneur de Langey, where there are everywhere things worthy to be known, and discourses above the vulgar strain."

---

[21] Martin du Bellay and Guillaume de Langey, brothers, who jointly wrote the Memoirs.

Of Cruelty

I FANCY virtue to be something else, and something more noble, than good nature, and the mere propension to goodness, that we are born into the world withal. Well-disposed and well-descended souls pursue, indeed, the same methods, and represent in their actions the same face that virtue itself does: but the word virtue imports, I know not what, more great and active than merely for a man to suffer himself, by a happy disposition, to be gently and quietly drawn to the rule of reason. He who, by a natural sweetness and facility, should despise injuries received, would, doubtless, do a very fine and laudable thing; but he who, provoked and nettled to the quick by an offence, should fortify himself with the arms of reason against the furious appetite of revenge, and, after a great conflict, master his own passion, would certainly do a great deal more. The first would do well; the latter virtuously: one action might be called goodness, and the other virtue; for, methinks, the very name of virtue presupposes difficulty and contention, and cannot be exercised without an opponent. 'Tis for this reason, perhaps, that we call God good, mighty, liberal, and just; but we do not call Him virtuous, being that all His operations are natural and without endeavour.[1] It has been the opinion of many philosophers, not only Stoics, but Epicureans — (and this addition[2] I borrow from the vulgar opinion, which is false, notwithstanding the witty conceit of Arcesilaus in answer to one, who, being reproached that many scholars went from his school to the Epicurean, but never any from thence to his school, said in answer, "I believe it indeed; numbers of capons being made out of

---

[1] Rousseau, in his "Emile," book v., adopts this passage, almost in the same words.

[2] "Montaigne stops here to make his excuse for thus naming the Epicureans with the Stoics, in conformity to the general opinion that the Epicureans were not so rigid in their morals as the Stoics, which is not true in the main, as he demonstrates at one view. This involved Montaigne in a tedious parenthesis, during which it is proper that the reader be attentive, that he may not entirely lose the thread of the argument. In some later editions of this author, it has been attempted to remedy this inconvenience, but without observing that Montaigne's argument is rendered more feeble and obscure by such vain repetitions: it is a licence that ought not to be taken, because he who publishes the work of another, ought to give it as the other composed it. But, in Mr. Cotton's translation, he was so puzzled with this enormous parenthesis that he has quite left it out." — Coste.

cocks, but never any cocks out of capons."[3] For, in truth, the Epicurean sect is not at all inferior to the Stoic in steadiness, and the rigour of opinions and precepts. And a certain Stoic, showing more honesty than those disputants, who, in order to quarrel with Epicurus, and to throw the game into their hands, make him say what he never thought, putting a wrong construction upon his words, clothing his sentences, by the strict rules of grammar, with another meaning, and a different opinion from that which they knew he entertained in his mind, and in his morals, the Stoic, I say, declared that he abandoned the Epicurean sect, upon this, among other considerations, that he thought their road too lofty and inaccessible; "Et ii qui φιλήδονοι vocantur sunt φιλόκαλοι et φιλοδίκαιοι, omnesque virtutes et colunt et retinent"[4]) — these philosophers say that it is not enough to have the soul seated in a good place, of a good temper, and well disposed to virtue; it is not enough to have our resolutions and our reasoning fixed above all the power of fortune, but that we are, moreover, to seek occasions wherein to put them to the proof: they would seek pain, necessity, and contempt, to contend with them and to keep the soul in breath: "Multum sibi adjicit virtus lacessita."[5] 'Tis one of the reasons why Epaminondas, who was yet of a third sect,[6] refused the riches fortune presented to him by very lawful means; because, said he, I am to contend with poverty, in which extreme he maintained himself to the last. Socrates put himself, methinks, upon a ruder trial, keeping for his exercise a confounded scolding wife, which was fighting at sharps. Metellus having, of all the Roman Senators, alone attempted, by the power of virtue, to withstand the violence of Saturninus, tribune of the people at Rome, who would, by all means, cause an unjust law to pass in favour of the commons, and, by so doing, having incurred the capital penalties that Saturninus had established against the dissentient, entertained those who, in this extremity, led him to execution with words to this effect: That it was a thing too easy and too base to do ill; and that to do well where there was no danger was a common thing; but that to do well where there was danger was the proper office of a man of virtue.[7] These words of Metellus very clearly represent to us what I would make out, viz., that virtue refuses facility for a companion; and that the easy, smooth, and descending way by which the regular steps of a sweet disposition of nature are conducted is not that of a true virtue; she requires a rough and stormy passage; she will have either exotic difficulties to wrestle with, like that of Metellus, by means whereof fortune delights to interrupt the speed of her career, or

---

[3] Diogenes Laertius, Life of Arcesilaus, lib. iv. § 43.

[4] "And those whom we call lovers of pleasure, being, in effect, lovers of honour and justice, cultivate and practise all the virtues." — Cicero, Ep. Fam. xv. 1, 19.

[5] "Virtue is much strengthened by combats." — Seneca, Ep. 13.

[6] The Pythagorean.

[7] Plutarch, Life of Marius, c. 10.

internal difficulties, that the inordinate appetites and imperfections of our condition introduce to disturb her.

I am come thus far at my ease; but here it comes into my head that the soul of Socrates, the most perfect that ever came to my knowledge, should, by this rule, be of very little recommendation; for I cannot conceive in that person any the least motion of a vicious inclination: I cannot imagine there could be any difficulty or constraint in the course of his virtue: I know his reason to be so powerful and sovereign over him that she would never have suffered a vicious appetite so much as to spring in him. To a virtue so elevated as his, I have nothing to oppose. Methinks I see him march, with a victorious and triumphant pace, in pomp and at his ease, without opposition or disturbance. If virtue cannot shine bright, but by the conflict of contrary appetites, shall we then say that she cannot subsist without the assistance of vice, and that it is from her that she derives her reputation and honour? What then, also, would become of that brave and generous Epicurean pleasure, which makes account that it nourishes virtue tenderly in her lap, and there makes it play and wanton, giving it for toys to play withal, shame, fevers, poverty, death, and torments? If I presuppose that a perfect virtue manifests itself in contending, in patient enduring of pain, and undergoing the uttermost extremity of the gout, without being moved in her seat; if I give her troubles and difficulty for her necessary objects: what will become of a virtue elevated to such a degree, as not only to despise pain, but, moreover, to rejoice in it, and to be tickled with the daggers of a sharp gout, such as the Epicureans have established, and of which many of them, by their actions, have given most manifest proofs? As have several others, who I find to have surpassed in effects even the very rules of their discipline; witness the younger Cato: when I see him die, and tearing out his own bowels, I am not satisfied simply to believe that he had then his soul totally exempt from all trouble and horror: I cannot think that he only maintained himself in the steadiness that the Stoical rules prescribed him; temperate, without emotion and imperturbed. There was, methinks, something in the virtue of this man too sprightly and fresh to stop there; I believe that, without doubt, he felt a pleasure and delight in so noble an action, and was more pleased in it than in any other of his life: "Sic abiit è vita, ut causam moriendi nactum se esse gauderet."[8] I believe it so thoroughly that I question whether he would have been content to have been deprived of the occasion of so brave an execution; and if the goodness that made him embrace the public concern more than his own, withheld me not, I should easily fall into an opinion that he thought himself obliged to fortune for having put his virtue upon so brave a trial, and for having favoured that thief[9] in

---

[8] "He quitted life, rejoicing that a reason for dying had arisen." — Cicero, Tusc. Quæs., i. 30.
[9] Cæsar.

treading underfoot the ancient liberty of his country. Methinks I read in
this action I know not what exaltation in his soul, and an extraordinary
and manly emotion of pleasure when he looked upon the generosity
and height of his enterprise:

"Deliberata morte ferocior,"[10]

not stimulated with any hope of glory, as the popular and effeminate
judgments of some have concluded (for that consideration was too
mean and low to possess so generous, so haughty, and so determined a
heart as his), but for the very beauty of the thing in itself, which he
who had the handling of the springs discerned more clearly and in its
perfection than we are able to do. Philosophy has obliged me in
determining that so brave an action had been indecently placed in any
other life than that of Cato; and that it only appertained to his to end
so; notwithstanding, and according to reason, he commanded his son
and the senators who accompanied him to take another course in their
affairs: "Catoni, quum incredibilem natura tribuisset gravitatem, eám-
que ipse perpetua constantia roboravisset, sempérque in proposito
consilio permansisset, moriendum potius, quàm tyranni vultus aspi-
ciendus, erat."[11] Every death ought to hold proportion with the life
before it; we do not become others for dying. I always interpret the
death by the life preceding; and if any one tell me of a death strong
and constant in appearance, annexed to a feeble life, I conclude it
produced by some feeble cause, and suitable to the life before. The
easiness then of this death and the facility of dying he had acquired by
the vigour of his soul; shall we say that it ought to abate anything of the
lustre of his virtue? And who, that has his brain never so little tinctured
with the true philosophy, can be content to imagine Socrates only free
from fear and passion in the accident of his prison, fetters and condemnation? and that will not discover in him not only firmness and
constancy (which was his ordinary condition), but, moreover, I know
not what new satisfaction, and a frolic cheerfulness in his last words
and actions? In the start he gave with the pleasure of scratching his leg
when his irons were taken off, does he not discover an equal serenity
and joy in his soul for being freed from past inconveniences, and at the
same time to enter into the knowledge of things to come? Cato shall
pardon me, if he please; his death indeed is more tragical and more
lingering; but yet this is, I know not how, methinks, finer. Aristippus, to
one that was lamenting this death: "The gods grant me such a one,"
said he.[12] A man discerns in the soul of these two great men and their

---

[10] "Bolder because he had determined to die." — Horace, Od. i. 37, 29.

[11] "Nature having endued Cato with an incredible gravity, which he had also fortified with a
perpetual constancy, without ever flagging in his resolution, he must of necessity rather die
than see the face of the tyrant." — Cicero, De Offic., i. 31.

[12] Diogenes Laertius, ii. 76.

imitators (for I very much doubt whether there were ever their equals) so perfect a habitude to virtue, that it was turned to a complexion. It is no longer a laborious virtue, nor the precepts of reason, to maintain which the soul is so racked, but the very essence of their soul, its natural and ordinary habit; they have rendered it such by a long practice of philosophical precepts having lit upon a rich and fine nature; the vicious passions that spring in us can find no entrance into them; the force and vigour of their soul stifle and extinguish irregular desires, so soon as they begin to move.

Now, that it is not more noble, by a high and divine resolution, to hinder the birth of temptations, and to be so formed to virtue, that the very seeds of vice are rooted out, than to hinder by main force their progress; and, having suffered ourselves to be surprised with the first motions of the passions, to arm ourselves and to stand firm to oppose their progress, and overcome them; and that this second effect is not also much more generous than to be simply endowed with a facile and affable nature, of itself disaffected to debauchery and vice, I do not think can be doubted; for this third and last sort of virtue seems to render a man innocent, but not virtuous; free from doing ill, but not apt enough to do well: considering also, that this condition is so near neighbour to imperfection and cowardice, that I know not very well how to separate the confines and distinguish them: the very names of goodness and innocence are, for this reason, in some sort grown into contempt. I very well know that several virtues, as chastity, sobriety, and temperance, may come to a man through personal defects. Constancy in danger, if it must be so called, the contempt of death, and patience in misfortunes, may ofttimes be found in men for want of well judging of such accidents, and not apprehending them for such as they are. Want of apprehension and stupidity sometimes counterfeit virtuous effects: as I have often seen it happen, that men have been commended for what really merited blame. An Italian lord once said this, in my presence, to the disadvantage of his own nation: that the subtlety of the Italians, and the vivacity of their conceptions were so great, and they foresaw the dangers and accidents that might befal them so far off, that it was not to be thought strange, if they were often, in war, observed to provide for their safety, even before they had discovered the peril; that we French and the Spaniards, who were not so cunning, went on further, and that we must be made to see and feel the danger before we would take the alarm; but that even then we could not stick to it. But the Germans and Swiss, more heavy and thick-skulled, had not the sense to look about them, even when the blows were falling about their ears. Peradventure, he only talked so for mirth's sake; and yet it is most certain that in war raw soldiers rush into danger with more precipitancy than after they have been well cudgelled:

> "Haud ignarus . . . quantum nova gloria in armis,
> Et prædulce decus, primo certamine, possit."[13]

For this reason it is that, when we judge of a particular action, we are to consider the circumstances, and the whole man by whom it is performed, before we give it a name.

To instance in myself: I have sometimes known my friends call that prudence in me, which was merely fortune; and repute that courage and patience, which was judgment and opinion; and attribute to me one title for another, sometimes to my advantage and sometimes otherwise. As to the rest, I am so far from being arrived at the first and most perfect degree of excellence, where virtue is turned into habit, that even of the second I have made no great proofs. I have not been very solicitous to curb the desires by which I have been importuned. My virtue is a virtue, or rather an innocence, casual and accidental. If I had been born of a more irregular complexion, I am afraid I should have made scurvy work; for I never observed any great stability in my soul to resist passions, if they were never so little vehement: I have not the knack of nourishing quarrels and debates in my own bosom, and, consequently, owe myself no great thanks that I am free from several vices.

> "Si vitiis mediocribus et mea paucis
> Mendosa est natura, alioqui recta; velut si
> Egregio inspersos reprehendas corpore nævos:"[14]

I owe it rather to my fortune than my reason. She has caused me to be descended of a race famous for integrity and of a very good father; I know not whether or no he has infused into me part of his humours, or whether domestic examples and the good education of my infancy have insensibly assisted in the work, or, if I was otherwise born so;

> "Seu Libra, seu me Scorpius adspicit
> Formidolosus, pars violentior,
>   Natalis horæ, seu tyrannus
>   Hesperiæ Capricornus undæ:"[15]

but so it is, that I have naturally a horror for most vices. The answer of Antisthenes to him who asked him, which was the best apprenticeship

---

[13] "Not ignorant, how hope of glory excites the young soldier in the first essay of arms." — Æneid, xi. 154.

[14] "If my nature be chargeable only with slight and few vices, and I am otherwise of rectitude, the venial faults will be no more than moles on a fair body." — Horatius, Sat. i. 6, 65.

[15] "Whether I was born under the Balance, or under Scorpio, formidable at the natal hour, or under Capricorn, ruler of the occidental seas." — Horace, Od. ii. 117.

"to unlearn evil," seems to point at this. I have them in horror, I say, with a detestation so natural, and so much my own, that the same instinct and impression I brought of them with me from my nurse, I yet retain, and no temptation whatever has had the power to make me alter it. Not so much as my own discourses, which in some things lashing out of the common road might seem easily to license me to actions that my natural inclination makes me hate. I will say a prodigious thing, but I will say it however: I find myself in many things more under reputation by my manners than by my opinion, and my concupiscence less debauched than my reason. Aristippus instituted opinions so bold in favour of pleasure and riches as set all the philosophers against him: but as to his manners, Dionysius the tyrant, having presented three beautiful women before him, to take his choice; he made answer, that he would choose them all, and that Paris got himself into trouble for having preferred one before the other two: but, having taken them home to his house, he sent them back untouched. His servant finding himself overladen upon the way, with the money he carried after him, he ordered him to pour out and throw away that which troubled him. And Epicurus, whose doctrines were so irreligious and effeminate, was in his life very laborious and devout; he wrote to a friend of his that he lived only upon biscuit and water, entreating him to send him a little cheese, to lie by him against he had a mind to make a feast.[16] Must it be true, that to be a perfect good man, we must be so by an occult, natural, and universal propriety, without law, reason, or example? The debauches wherein I have been engaged, have not been, I thank God, of the worst sort, and I have condemned them in myself, for my judgment was never infected by them; on the contrary, I accuse them more severely in myself than in any other; but that is all, for, as to the rest, I oppose too little resistance and suffer myself to incline too much to the other side of the balance, excepting that I moderate them, and prevent them from mixing with other vices, which, for the most part will cling together, if a man have not a care. I have contracted and curtailed mine, to make them as single and as simple as I can:

> "Nec ultra
> Errorem foveo."[17]

For as to the opinion of the Stoics, who say, "That the wise man when he works, works by all the virtues together, though one be most apparent, according to the nature of the action;" and herein the similitude of a human body might serve them somewhat, for the action of anger cannot

---

[16] Diogenes Laertius, x. 11.
[17] "Nor carry wrong further."— Juvenal, viii. 164.

work unless all the humours assist it, though choler predominate; — if they will thence draw a like consequence, that when the wicked man does wickedly, he does it by all the vices together, I do not believe it to be so, or else I understand them not, for I by effect find the contrary. These are sharp, unsubstantial subtleties, with which philosophy sometimes amuses itself. I follow some vices, but I fly others as much as a saint would do. The Peripatetics also disown this indissoluble connection; and Aristotle is of opinion that a prudent and just man may be intemperate and inconsistent. Socrates confessed to some who had discovered a certain inclination to vice in his physiognomy, that it was, in truth, his natural propension, but that he had by discipline corrected it.[18] And such as were familiar with the philosopher Stilpo said, that being born with addiction to wine and women, he had by study rendered himself very abstinent both from the one and the other.[19]

What I have in me of good, I have, quite contrary, by the chance of my birth; and hold it not either by law, precept, or any other instruction: the innocence that is in me is a simple one; little vigour and no art. Amongst other vices, I mortally hate cruelty, both by nature and judgment, as the very extreme of all vices: nay, with so much tenderness that I cannot see a chicken's neck pulled off, without trouble, and cannot, without impatience, endure the cry of a hare in my dog's teeth, though the chase be a violent pleasure. Such as have sensuality to encounter, freely make use of this argument, to show that it is altogether "vicious and unreasonable; that when it is at the height, it masters us to that degree that a man's reason can have no access,"[20] and instance our own experience in the act of love,

> "Quum jam præsagit guadia corpus,
> Atque in eo est Venus, ut muliebria conserat arva."[21]

wherein they conceive that the pleasure so transports us, that our reason cannot perform its office, whilst we are in such ecstacy and rapture. I know very well it may be otherwise, and that a man may sometimes, if he will, gain this point over himself to sway his soul, even in the critical moment, to think of something else; but then he must ply it to that bent. I know that a man may triumph over the utmost effort of this pleasure: I have experienced it in myself, and have not found Venus so imperious a goddess, as many, and much more virtuous men than I, declare. I do not consider it a miracle, as the Queen of Navarre does in one of the tales of

---

[18] Cicero, Tusc. Quæs., iv. 27.

[19] Idem, De Fato, c. 5.

[20] Idem, De Senect., c. 12.

[21] Lucretius, iv. 1099. The sense is in the preceding passage of the text.

her Heptameron (which is a very pretty book of that kind) nor for a thing of extreme difficulty, to pass whole nights, where a man has all the convenience and liberty he can desire, with a long-coveted mistress, and yet be true to the pledge first given to satisfy himself with kisses and suchlike endearments, without pressing any further. I conceive that the example of the pleasure of the chase would be more proper; wherein though the pleasure be less, there is the higher excitement of unexpected joy, giving no time for the reason, taken by surprise, to prepare itself for the encounter, when after a long quest the beast starts up on a sudden in a place where, peradventure, we least expected it; the shock and the ardour of the shouts and cries of the hunters so strike us, that it would be hard for those who love this lesser chase, to turn their thoughts, upon the instant, another way; and the poets make Diana triumph over the torch and shafts of Cupid:

> "Quis non malarum, quas amor curas habet,
> Hæc inter obliviscitur?"[22]

To return to what I was saying before, I am tenderly compassionate of others' afflictions, and should readily cry for company, if, upon any occasion whatever, I could cry at all. Nothing tempts my tears, but tears, and not only those that are real and true, but whatever they are, feigned or painted. I do not much lament the dead, and should envy them rather; but I very much lament the dying. The savages do not so much offend me, in roasting and eating the bodies of the dead, as they do who torment and persecute the living. Nay, I cannot look so much as upon the ordinary executions of justice, how reasonable soever, with a steady eye. Some one having to give testimony of Julius Cæsar's clemency; "he was," says he, "mild in his revenges. Having compelled the pirates to yield by whom he had before been taken prisoner and put to ransom; forasmuch as he had threatened them with the cross, he indeed condemned them to it, but it was after they had been first strangled. He punished his secretary Philemon, who had attempted to poison him, with no greater severity than mere death." Without naming that Latin author,[23] who thus dares to allege as a testimony of mercy the killing only of those by whom we have been offended, it is easy to guess that he was struck with the horrid and inhuman examples of cruelty practised by the Roman tyrants.

For my part, even in justice itself, all that exceeds a simple death appears to me pure cruelty; especially in us who ought, having regard to

---

[22] "Who, amongst such delights, would not remove out of his thoughts the anxious cares of love?" — Horace, Epod., ii. 37.

[23] Suetonius, Life of Cæsar, c. 74.

their souls, to dismiss them in a good and calm condition; which cannot be, when we have agitated them by insufferable torments. Not long since, a soldier who was a prisoner, perceiving from a tower where he was shut up, that the people began to assemble to the place of execution, and that the carpenters were busy erecting a scaffold, he presently concluded that the preparation was for him; and therefore entered into a resolution to kill himself, but could find no instrument to assist him in his design except an old rusty cart-nail that fortune presented to him; with this he first gave himself two great wounds about his throat, but finding these would not do, he presently afterwards gave himself a third in the belly, where he left the nail sticking up to the head. The first of his keepers who came in found him in this condition: yet alive, but sunk down and exhausted by his wounds. To make use of time, therefore, before he should die, they made haste to read his sentence; which having done, and he hearing that he was only condemned to be be-headed, he seemed to take new courage, accepted wine which he had before refused, and thanked his judges for the unhoped-for mildness of their sentence; saying, that he had taken a resolution to despatch him-self for fear of a more severe and insupportable death, having enter-tained an opinion, by the preparations he had seen in the place, that they were resolved to torment him with some horrible execution, and seemed to be delivered from death, in having it changed from what he apprehended.

I should advise that those examples of severity, by which 'tis designed to retain the people in their duty, might be exercised upon the dead bodies of criminals; for to see them deprived of sepulture, to see them boiled and divided into quarters, would almost work as much upon the vulgar, as the pain they make the living endure; though that in effect be little or nothing, as God himself says, "Who kill the body, and, after that, have no more that they can do;"[24] and the poets singularly dwell upon the horrors of this picture, as something worse than death:

> "Heu! reliquias semiassi regis, denudatis ossibus,
> Per terram sanie delibutas fœde divexarier."[25]

I happened to come by one day, accidentally, at Rome, just as they were upon executing Catena, a notorious robber: he was strangled without any emotion of the spectators, but when they came to cut him in quarters, the hangman gave not a blow that the people did not follow with a doleful cry and exclamation, as if every one had lent his sense of

---

[24] Luke xii. 4.

[25] "Alas! that the half-burnt remains of these kings, and their bared bones, should be shamefully dragged through the dirt." — Cicero, Tusc. Quæs., i. 44.

feeling to the miserable carcase. Those inhuman excesses ought to be exercised upon the bark, and not upon the quick. Artaxerxes, in almost a like case, moderated the severity of the ancient laws of Persia, ordaining that the nobility who had committed a fault, instead of being whipped, as they were used to be, should be stripped only and their clothes whipped for them; and that whereas they were wont to tear off their hair, they should only take off their high-crowned tiara.[26] The so devout Egyptians thought they sufficiently satisfied the divine justice by sacrificing hogs in effigy and representation; a bold invention to pay God, so essential a substance, in picture only and in show.

I live in a time wherein we abound in incredible examples of this vice, through the licence of our civil wars; and we see nothing in ancient histories more extreme than what we have proof of every day, but I cannot, any the more, get used to it. I could hardly persuade myself, before I saw it with my eyes, that there could be found souls so cruel and fell, who, for the sole pleasure of murder, would commit it; would hack and lop off the limbs of others; sharpen their wits to invent unusual torments and new kinds of death, without hatred, without profit, and for no other end but only to enjoy the pleasant spectacle of the gestures and motions, the lamentable groans and cries of a man dying in anguish. For this is the utmost point to which cruelty can arrive: "Ut homo hominem, non iratus, non timens, tantum spectaturus, occidat."[27] For my own part, I cannot without grief see so much as an innocent beast pursued and killed that has no defence, and from which we have received no offence at all; and that which frequently happens, that the stag we hunt, finding himself weak and out of breath, and seeing no other remedy, surrenders himself to us who pursue him, imploring mercy by his tears

"Questuque cruentus,
Atque imploranti similis,"[28]

has ever been to me a very unpleasing sight; and I hardly ever take a beast alive that I do not presently turn out again. Pythagoras bought them of fishermen and fowlers to do the same:

"Primoque a cæde ferarum,
Incaluisse puto maculatum sanguine ferrum."[29]

---

[26] Plutarch, Notable Sayings of the Ancient Kings.

[27] "That a man should kill a man without being angry, or without fear, only for the pleasure of the spectacle." — Seneca, Ep., 90.

[28] "Who, bleeding, by his tears seems to crave mercy." — Æneid, vii. 501.

[29] "I think 'twas slaughter of wild beasts that first stained the steel of man with blood." — Ovid, Met., xv. 106.

Those natures that are sanguinary towards beasts discover a natural propension to cruelty. After they had accustomed themselves at Rome to spectacles of the slaughter of animals, they proceeded to those of the slaughter of men, to the gladiators. Nature has herself, I fear, imprinted in man a kind of instinct to inhumanity; nobody takes pleasure in seeing beasts play with and caress one another, but every one is delighted with seeing them dismember, and tear one another to pieces. And that I may not be laughed at for the sympathy I have with them, theology itself enjoins us some favour in their behalf; and considering that one and the same master has lodged us together in this palace for his service, and that they, as well as we, are of his family, it has reason to enjoin us some affection and regard to them. Pythagoras borrowed the metempsychosis from the Egyptians; but it has since been received by several nations, and particularly by our Druids:

> "Morte carent animæ; semperque, priore relicta
> Sede, novis domibus vivunt, habitantque receptæ."[30]

The religion of our ancient Gauls maintained that souls, being eternal, never ceased to remove and shift their places from one body to another; mixing moreover with this fancy some consideration of divine justice; for according to the deportments of the soul, whilst it had been in Alexander, they said that God assigned it another body to inhabit, more or less painful, and proper for its condition:

> "Muta ferarum
> Cogit vincla pati; truculentos ingerit ursis,
> Prædonesque lupis; fallaces vulpibus addit:
> Atque ubi per varios annos, per mille figuras
> Egit, Lethæo purgatos flumine, tandem
> Rursus ad humanæ revocat primordia formæ:"[31]

if it had been valiant, he lodged it in the body of a lion; if voluptuous, in that of hog; if timorous, in that of a hart or hare; if malicious, in that of a fox, and so of the rest, till having purified it by this chastisement, it again entered into the body of some other man:

> "Ipse ego, nam memini, Trojani tempore belli
> Panthoides Euphorbus eram."[32]

---

[30] "Souls never die, but, having left one seat, are received into new houses." — Ovid, Met., xv. 158.

[31] "He made them wear the silent chains of brutes, the bloodthirsty souls he enclosed in bears; the thieves in wolves; the sly in foxes; where after having, through successive years and a thousand forms, finished these careers, purging them well in Lethe's flood, at last he replaces them in human bodies." — Claudian, Contra Ruf., ii. 482.

[32] "For I myself remember that in the days of the Trojan war, I was Euphorbus, son of Pantheus." — Ovid, Met., xv. 160; and see Diogenes Laertius, Life of Pythagoras.

As to the relationship betwixt us and beasts, I do not much admit of it; nor of that which several nations, and those among the most ancient and most noble, have practised, who have not only received brutes into their society and companionship, but have given them a rank infinitely above themselves, esteeming them one while familiars and favourites of the gods, and having them in more than human, reverence and respect; others acknowledged no other god or divinity than they. "Belluæ à barbaris propter beneficium consecratæ:"[33]

> "Crocodilon adorat
> Pars hæc; illa pavet saturam serpentibus ibin:
> Effigies sacri hic nitet aurea cercopitheci;
>   Hic piscem fluminis, illic
> Oppida tota canem venerantur."[34]

And the very interpretation that Plutarch[35] gives to this error, which is very well conceived, is advantageous to them: for he says that it was not the cat or the ox, for example, that the Egyptians adored: but that they, in those beasts, adored some image of the divine faculties; in this, patience and utility; in that vivacity, or, as with our neighbours the Burgundians and all the Germans, impatience to see themselves shut up; by which they represented liberty, which they loved and adored above all other godlike attributes, and so of the rest. But when, amongst the more moderate opinions, I meet with arguments that endeavour to demonstrate the near resemblance betwixt us and animals, how large a share they have in our greatest privileges, and with how much probability they compare us together, truly I abate a great deal of our presumption, and willingly resign that imaginary sovereignty that is attributed to us over other creatures.

But supposing all this were not true, there is, nevertheless, a certain respect, a general duty of humanity, not only to beasts that have life and sense but even to trees and plants. We owe justice to men, and graciousness and benignity to other creatures that are capable of it; there is a certain commerce and mutual obligation betwixt them and us. Nor shall I be afraid to confess the tenderness of my nature so childish, that I cannot well refuse to play with my dog, when he the most unseasonably importunes me so to do. The Turks have alms and hospitals for beasts. The Romans had public care to the nourishment of geese, by whose vigilance their Capitol had been preserved. The Athenians made a

---

[33] "The barbarians consecrated beasts, out of opinion of some benefit received by them." — Cicero, De Natura Deor. i. 36.

[34] "This place adores the crocodile; another dreads the ibis, feeder on serpents; here you may behold the statue of a monkey shining in gold; here men venerate a river fish; there whole towns worship a dog." — Juvenal, xv. 2.

[35] On Isis and Osiris, c. 39.

decree that the mules and moyls which had served at the building of the
temple called Hecatompedon should be free and suffered to pasture at
their own choice, without hindrance.[36] The Agrigentines[37] had a common use solemnly to inter the beasts they had a kindness for, as horses of
some rare quality, dogs, and useful birds, and even those that had only
been kept to divert their children; and the magnificence that was ordinary with them in all other things, also particularly appeared in the
sumptuosity and numbers of monuments erected to this end, and which
remained in their beauty several ages after. The Egyptians[38] buried
wolves, bears, crocodiles, dogs, and cats in sacred places, embalmed
their bodies, and put on mourning at their death. Cimon gave an
honourable sepulture to the mares with which he had three times
gained the prize of the course at the Olympic Games.[39] The ancient
Xantippus caused his dog to be interred on an eminence near the sea,
which has ever since retained the name,[40] and Plutarch says, that he
had a scruple about selling for a small profit to the slaughterer an ox that
had been long in his service.[41]

---

[36] Plutarch, Life of Cato the Censor, c. 3.

[37] Diogenes, Siculus, xiii. 17.

[38] Idem, ibid.

[39] Herodotus, book ii.

[40] Plutarch, *ut supra.*

[41] Idem, ibid.

Of Repentance

OTHERS FORM MAN; I only report him: and represent a particular one, ill fashioned enough, and whom, if I had to model him anew, I should certainly make something else than what he is: but that's past recalling. Now, though the features of my picture alter and change, 'tis not, however, unlike: the world eternally turns round; all things therein are incessantly moving, the earth, the rocks of Caucasus, and the Pyramids of Egypt, both by the public motion and their own. Even constancy itself is no other but a slower and more languishing motion. I cannot fix my object; 'tis always tottering and reeling by a natural giddiness: I take it as it is at the instant I consider it; I do not paint its being, I paint its passage; not a passing from one age to another, or, as the people say, from seven to seven years, but from day to day, from minute to minute. I must accommodate my history to the hour: I may presently change, not only by fortune, but also by intention. 'Tis a counterpart of various and changeable accidents, and of irresolute imaginations, and, as it falls out, sometimes contrary: whether it be that I am then another self, or that I take subjects by other circumstances and considerations: so it is, that I may peradventure contradict myself, but, as Demades said, I never contradict the truth. Could my soul once take footing, I would not essay but resolve: but it is always learning and making trial.

I propose a life ordinary and without lustre: 'tis all one; all moral philosophy may as well be applied to a common and private life, as to one of richer composition: every man carries the entire form of human condition. Authors communicate themselves to the people by some especial and extrinsic mark; I, the first of any, by my universal being; as Michael de Montaigne, not as a grammarian, a poet, or a lawyer. If the world find fault that I speak too much of myself, I find fault that they do not so much as think of themselves. But is it reason, that being so particular in my way of living, I should pretend to recommend myself to the public knowledge? And is it also reason that I should produce to the world, where art and handling have so much credit and authority, crude and simple effects of nature, and of a weak nature to boot? Is it not to build a wall without stone or brick, or some such thing, to write books without learning and without art? The fancies of music are carried on by art; mine by chance. I have this, at least, according to discipline, that never any man treated of a subject he better understood and knew, than I what I have undertaken, and that in this I am the most understanding man alive: secondly, that never any man penetrated farther into his matter, nor better and more distinctly sifted the parts and sequences of it, nor ever more exactly and fully arrived at the end he proposed to himself. To perfect it, I need bring nothing but fidelity to the work; and that is there, and the most pure and sincere that is anywhere to be found. I speak truth, not so much as I would, but as much as I dare; and I dare a little the more, as I grow older; for, methinks, custom allows to age more liberty of prating, and more indiscretion of talking of a man's self. That cannot fall out here, which I often see elsewhere, that the work and the artificer contradict one another: "can a man of such sober conversation have written so foolish a book?" Or "do so learned writings proceed from a man of so weak conversation?" He who talks at a very ordinary rate, and writes rare matter, 'tis to say that his capacity is borrowed and not his own. A learned man is not learned in all things: but a sufficient man is sufficient throughout, even to ignorance itself; here my book and I go hand in hand together. Elsewhere men may commend or censure the work, without reference to the workman; here they cannot: who touches the one, touches the other. He who shall judge of it without knowing him, will more wrong himself than me; he who does know him, gives me all the satisfaction I desire. I shall be happy beyond my desert, if I can obtain only thus much from the public approbation, as to make men of understanding perceive that I was capable of profiting by knowledge, had I had it; and that I deserved to have been assisted by a better memory.

Be pleased here to excuse what I often repeat, that I very rarely repent, and that my conscience is satisfied with itself, not as the conscience of an angel, or that of a horse, but as the conscience of a man; always adding this clause, not one of ceremony, but a true and real submission, that I speak inquiring and doubting, purely and simply referring myself to the common and accepted beliefs for the resolution. I do not teach, I only relate.

There is no vice that is absolutely a vice which does not offend, and that a sound judgment does not accuse; for there is in it so manifest a deformity and inconvenience, that, peradventure, they are in the right who say that it is chiefly begotten by stupidity and ignorance: so hard is it to imagine that a man can know without abhorring it. Malice sucks up the greatest part of its own venom, and poisons itself.[1] Vice leaves repentance in the soul, like an ulcer in the flesh, which is always scratching and lacerating itself: for reason effaces all other grief and sorrows, but it begets that of repentance, which is so much the more grievous, by reason it springs within, as the cold and heat of fevers are more sharp than those that only strike upon the outward skin. I hold for vices (but every one according to its proportion), not only those which reason and nature condemn, but those also which the opinion of men, though false and erroneous, have made such, if authorised by law and custom.

There is likewise no virtue which does not rejoice a well-descended nature; there is a kind of, I know not what, congratulation in well doing that gives us an inward satisfaction, and a generous boldness that accompanies a good conscience: a soul daringly vicious may, peradventure, arm itself with security, but it cannot supply itself with this complacency and satisfaction. 'Tis no little satisfaction to feel a man's self preserved from the contagion of so depraved an age, and to say to himself: "Whoever could penetrate into my soul would not there find me guilty either of the affliction or ruin of any one, or of revenge or envy, or any offence against the public laws, or of innovation or disturbance, or failure of my word; and though the licence of the time permits and teaches every one so to do, yet have I not plundered any Frenchman's goods, or taken his money, and have lived upon what is my own, in war as well as in peace; neither have I set any man to work without paying him his hire." These testimonies of a good conscience please, and this natural rejoicing is very beneficial to us, and the only reward that we can never fail of.

To ground the recompense of virtuous actions upon the approbation of others is too uncertain and unsafe a foundation, especially in so corrupt and ignorant an age as this, wherein the good opinion of the vulgar is injurious: upon whom do you rely to show you what is recommendable? God defend me from being an honest man, according to the descriptions of honour I daily see every one make of himself. "Quæ fuerant vitia, mores sunt."[2] Some of my friends have at times schooled and scolded me with great sincerity and plainness, either of their own voluntary motion, or by me entreated to it as to an office, which to a well-composed soul surpasses not only in utility, but in kindness, all other offices of friendship: I have always received them with the most open arms, both of courtesy and acknowledgment; but, to say the truth, I have often found so much false measure, both in their reproaches and praises, that I had not done much amiss, rather to have done ill, than to have done well according to their notions. We,

---

[1] Seneca, Ep. 81.

[2] "What before were vices are now right manners." — Seneca, Ep. 39.

who live private lives, not exposed to any other view than our own, ought chiefly to have settled a pattern within ourselves by which to try our actions; and according to that, sometimes to encourage and sometimes to correct ourselves. I have my laws and my judicature to judge of myself, and apply myself more to these than to any other rules: I do, indeed, restrain my actions according to others; but extend them not by any other rule than my own. You yourself only know if you are cowardly and cruel, loyal and devout: others see you not, and only guess at you by uncertain conjectures, and do not so much see your nature as your art; rely not therefore upon their opinions, but stick to your own: "Tuo tibi judicio est utendum . . . Virtutis et vitiorum grave ipsius conscientiæ pondus est: qua sublata, jacent omnia."[3]

But the saying that repentance immediately follows the sin seems not to have respect to sin in its high estate, which is lodged in us as in its own proper habitation. One may disown and retract the vices that surprise us, and to which we are hurried by passions; but those which by a long habit are rooted in a strong and vigorous will are not subject to contradiction. Repentance is no other but a recanting of the will and an opposition to our fancies, which lead us which way they please. It makes this person disown his former virtue and continency:

> "Quæ mens est hodie, cur eadem non puero fuit?
> Vel cur his animis incolumes non redeunt genæ?"[4]

'Tis an exact life that maintains itself in due order in private. Every one may juggle his part, and represent an honest man upon the stage: but within, and in his own bosom, where all may do as they list, where all is concealed, to be regular — there's the point. The next degree is to be so in his house, and in his ordinary actions, for which we are accountable to none, and where there is no study nor artifice. And therefore Bias, setting forth the excellent state of a private family, says: "of which[5] the master is the same within, by his own virtue and temper that, he is abroad, for fear of the laws and report of men." And it was a worthy saying of Julius Drusus,[6] to the masons who offered him, for three thousand crowns, to put his house in such a posture that his

---

[3] "Thou must employ thy own judgment upon thyself; great is the weight of thy own conscience in the discovery of thy own virtues and vices: that being taken away, all things are lost."—Cicero, De Nat. Dei, iii. 35; Tusc. Quæs., i. 25.

[4] "Why was I not of the same mind when I was a boy that I am now? or why do not the ruddy cheeks of my youth return to help me now." — Horace, Od. iv. 10, 7.

[5] Plutarch, Banquet of the Seven Sages.

[6] He is called so by Plutarch in his Instructions to Those Who Manage State Affairs, but he was, in reality, Marcus Livius Drusus, the famous tribune, as we find in Paterculus.

neighbours should no longer have the same inspection into it as before; "I will give you," said he, "six thousand to make it so that everybody may see into every room." 'Tis honourably recorded of Agesilaus,[7] that he used in his journeys always to take up his lodgings in temples, to the end that the people and the gods themselves might pry into his most private actions. Such a one has been a miracle to the world, in whom neither his wife nor servant has ever seen anything so much as remarkable; few men have been admired by their own domestics; no one was ever a prophet, not merely in his own house, but in his own country, says the experience of histories: 'tis the same in things of nought, and in this low example the image of a greater is to be seen. In my country of Gascony, they look upon it as a drollery to see me in print; the further off I am read from my own home, the better I am esteemed. I am fain to purchase printers in Guienne; elsewhere they purchase me. Upon this it is that they lay their foundation who conceal themselves present and living, to obtain a name when they are absent and dead. I had rather have a great deal less in hand, and do not expose myself to the world upon any other account than my present share; when I leave it I quit the rest. See this functionary whom the people escort in state, with wonder and applause, to his very door; he puts off the pageant with his robe, and falls so much the lower by how much he was higher exalted: in himself within, all is tumult and degraded. And though all should be regular there, it will require a vivid and well-chosen judgment to perceive it in these low and private actions; to which may be added, that order is a dull, sombre virtue. To enter a breach, conduct an embassy, govern a people, are actions of renown: to reprehend, laugh, sell, pay, love, hate, and gently and justly converse with a man's own family, and with himself; not to relax, not to give a man's self the lie, is more rare and hard, and less remarkable. By which means, retired lives, whatever is said to the contrary, undergo duties of as great or greater difficulty than the others do; and private men, says Aristotle,[8] serve virtue more painfully and highly, than those in authority do: we prepare ourselves for eminent occasions, more out of glory than conscience. The shortest way to arrive at glory, would be to do that for conscience which we do for glory: and the virtue of Alexander appears to me of much less vigour in his great theatre, than that of Socrates in his mean and obscure employment. I can easily conceive Socrates in the place of Alexander, but Alexander in that of Socrates, I cannot. Who shall ask the one what he can do, he will answer, Subdue the world: and who shall put the same question to the other, he will say, "Carry on human life conformably

---

[7] Plutarch, in vita, c. 5.

[8] Moral. ad Nicom., x. 7.

with its natural condition;"9 a much more general, weighty, and legitimate science than the other.

The virtue of the soul does not consist in flying high, but in walking orderly; its grandeur does not exercise itself in grandeur, but in mediocrity. As they who judge and try us within, make no great account of the lustre of our public actions, and see they are only streaks and rays of clear water springing from a slimy and muddy bottom: so, likewise, they who judge of us by this gallant outward appearance, in like manner conclude of our internal constitution; and cannot couple common faculties, and like their own, with the other faculties that astonish them, and are so far out of their sight. Therefore it is, that we give such savage forms to demons: and who does not give Tamerlane great eye-brows, wide nostrils, a dreadful visage, and a prodigious stature, according to the imagination he has conceived by the report of his name? Had any one formerly brought me to Erasmus, I should hardly have believed but that all was adage and apothegm he spoke to his man or his hostess. We much more aptly imagine an artisan upon his close-stool, or upon his wife, than a great president venerable by his port and sufficiency: we fancy that they, from their high tribunals, will not abase themselves so much as to live. As vicious souls are often incited by some foreign impulse to do well, so are virtuous souls to do ill; they are therefore to be judged by their settled state, when they are at home, whenever that may be; and, at all events, when they are nearer repose, and in their native station.

Natural inclinations are much assisted and fortified by education; but they seldom alter and overcome their institution: a thousand natures of my time have escaped towards virtue or vice, through a quite contrary discipline;

> "Sic ubi desuetæ silvis in carcere clausæ
> Mansuevere feræ, et vultus posuere minaces,
> Atque hominem didicere pati, si torrida parvus
> Venit in ora cruor, redeunt rabiesque furorque,
> Admonitæque tument gustato sanguine fauces;
> Fervet, et a trepido vix abstinet ira magistro;"10

these original qualities are not to be rooted out; they may be covered and concealed. The Latin tongue is as it were natural to me; I understand it

---

9 Montaigne added here, "To do for the world that for which he came into the world," but he afterwards erased these words from the manuscript. — Naigeon.

10 "So savage beasts, when shut up in cages, and grown unaccustomed to the woods, become tame, and lay aside their fierce looks, and submit to the rule of man; if again they taste blood, their rage and fury return, their jaws are erected by thirst of blood, and they scarcely forbear to assail their trembling masters." — Lucan, iv. 237.

better than French; but I have not been used to speak it, nor hardly to write it these forty years. Yet, upon extreme and sudden emotions which I have fallen into twice or thrice in my life, and once, seeing my father in perfect health fall upon me in a swoon, I have always uttered my first outcries and ejaculations in Latin; nature starting up, and forcibly expressing itself, in spite of so long a discontinuation; and this example is said of many others.

They who in my time have attempted to correct the manners of the world by new opinions, reform seeming vices, but the essential vices they leave as they were, if, indeed, they do not augment them; and augmentation is, therein, to be feared; we defer all other well doing upon the account of these external reformations, of less cost and greater show, and thereby expiate good cheap, for the other natural, consubstantial and intestine vices. Look a little into our experience: there is no man, if he listen to himself, who does not in himself discover a particular and governing form of his own, that jostles his education, and wrestles with the tempest of passions that are contrary to it. For my part, I seldom find myself agitated with surprises; I always find myself in my place, as heavy and unwieldy bodies do; if I am not at home, I am always near at hand; my dissipations do not transport me very far, there is nothing strange or extreme in the case; and yet I have sound and vigorous turns.

The true condemnation, and which touches the common practice of men, is, that their very retirement itself is full of filth and corruption; the idea of their reformation composed; their repentance sick and faulty, very nearly as much as their sin. Some, either from having been linked to vice by a natural propension, or long practice, cannot see its deformity. Others (of which constitution I am) do indeed feel the weight of vice, but they counter-balance it with pleasure, or some other occasion; and suffer, and lend themselves to it, for a certain price, but viciously and basely. Yet there might, haply, be imagined so vast a disproportion of measure, where with justice the pleasure might excuse the sin, as we say of utility; not only if accidental, and out of sin, as in thefts, but in the very exercise of sin, as in the enjoyment of women, where the temptation is violent, and 'tis said, sometimes not to be overcome.

Being the other day at Armaignac, on the estate of a kinsman of mine, I there saw a country fellow who was by every one nicknamed the thief. He thus related the story of his life: that being born a beggar, and finding that he should not be able, so as to be clear of indigence, to get his living by the sweat of his brow, he resolved to turn thief, and by means of his strength of body, had exercised this trade all the time of his youth in great security; for he ever made his harvest and vintage in other men's grounds, but a great way off, and in so great quantities, that it was not to be imagined one man could have carried away so much in one night upon his shoulders; and, moreover, was careful equally to divide and distribute the mischief he did, that the loss was of less importance to every particular man. He is now grown old, and rich for a man of his condition, thanks to his trade, which he openly confesses to every one. And to make his peace with God, he says, that he is daily ready by good offices to make satisfaction to the successors of those he has robbed, and if he do not finish (for to do it all at once he is not able) he will then leave it in charge to his heirs to perform the rest, proportionably to the wrong he himself only knows he has done to each. By this description, true or false, this man looks upon theft as a dishonest action, and hates it, but less than poverty, and simply repents; but to the extent he has thus recompensed, he repents not. This is not that habit which incorporates us into vice, and conforms even our understanding itself to it; nor is it that impetuous whirlwind that by gusts troubles and blinds our souls, and for the time precipitates us, judgment and all, into the power of vice.

I customarily do what I do thoroughly and make but one step on't; I have rarely any movement that hides itself and steals away from my reason, and that does not proceed in the matter by the consent of all my faculties, without division or intestine sedition; my judgment is to have all the blame or all the praise; and the blame it once has, it has always; for almost from my infancy it has ever been one: the same inclination, the same turn, the same force: and as to universal opinions, I fixed myself from my childhood in the place where I resolved to stick. There are some sins that are impetuous, prompt, and sudden; let us set them aside; but in these other sins so often repeated, deliberated, and contrived, whether sins of complexion or sins of profession and vocation, I cannot conceive that they should have so long been settled in the same resolution, unless the reason and conscience of him who has them, be constant to have them; and the repentance he boasts to be inspired with on a sudden, is very hard for me to imagine or form. I follow not the opinion of the Pythagorean sect, "that men take up a new soul when they repair to the images of the gods to receive their oracles," unless he mean that it must needs be extrinsic, new, and lent for the time; our own showing so little sign of purification and cleanness, fit for such an office.

They act quite contrary to the stoical precepts, who do indeed, command us to correct the imperfections and vices we know ourselves guilty of, but forbid us therefore to disturb the repose of our souls: these make us believe that they have great grief and remorse within: but of amendment, correction, or interruption, they make nothing appear. It cannot be a cure if the malady be not wholly discharged; if repentance were laid upon the scale of the balance, it would weigh down sin. I find no quality so easy to counterfeit as devotion, if men do not conform their manners and life to the profession; its essence is abstruse and occult; the appearances easy and ostentatious.

For my own part, I may desire in general to be other than I am; I may condemn and dislike my whole form, and beg of Almighty God for an entire reformation, and that He will please to pardon my natural infirmity: but I ought not to call this repentance, methinks, no more than the being dissatisfied that I am not an angel or Cato. My actions are regular, and conformable with what I am, and to my condition; I can do no better; and repentance does not properly touch things that are not in our power; sorrow does. I imagine an infinite number of natures more elevated and regular than mine; and yet I do not for all that improve my faculties, no more than my arm or will grow more strong and vigorous for conceiving those of another to be so. If to conceive and wish a nobler way of acting than that we have, should produce a repentance of our own, we must then repent us of our most innocent actions, forasmuch as we may well suppose that in a more excellent nature they would have been carried on with greater dignity and perfection; and we would that ours were so. When I reflect upon the deportments of my youth, with that of my old age, I find that I have commonly behaved myself with equal order in both, according to what I understand: this is all that my resistance can do. I do not flatter myself; in the same circumstances I should do the same things. It is not a patch, but rather an universal tincture, with which I am stained. I know no repentance, superficial, half-way, and ceremonious; it must sting me all over before I can call it so, and must prick my bowels as deeply and universally as God sees into me.

As to business, many excellent opportunities have escaped me for want of good management; and yet my deliberations were sound enough, according to the occurrences presented to me: 'tis their way to choose always the easiest and safest course. I find that, in my former resolves, I have proceeded with discretion, according to my own rule, and according to the state of the subject proposed, and should do the same a thousand years hence in like occasions; I do not consider what it is now, but what it was then, when I deliberated on it: the force of all counsel consists in the time; occasions and things eternally shift and change. I have in my life committed some important errors, not for want of good understanding, but for want of good luck. There are secret, and not to be foreseen, parts in matters we have in hand, especially in the nature of men; mute conditions, that make no show, unknown sometimes even to the possessors themselves, that spring and start up by incidental occasions; if my prudence could not penetrate into nor foresee them, I blame it not: 'tis commissioned no further than its own limits; if the event be too hard for me, and take the side I have refused, there is no remedy; I do not blame myself, I accuse my fortune, and not my work; this cannot be called repentance.

Phocion, having given the Athenians an advice that was not followed, and the affair nevertheless succeeding contrary to his opinion, some one said to him; "Well, Phocion, art thou content that matters go so well?" "I am very well content," replied he, "that this has happened so well, but I do not repent that I counselled the other."[11] When any of my friends address themselves to me for advice, I give it candidly and clearly, without sticking, as almost all other men do, at the hazard of the thing's falling out contrary to my opinion, and that I may be reproached for my counsel; I am very indifferent as to that, for the fault will be theirs for having consulted me, and I could not refuse them that office.

I, for my own part, can rarely blame anyone but myself for my oversights and misfortunes, for indeed I seldom solicit the advice of another, if not by honour of ceremony, or excepting where I stand in need of information, special science, or as to matter of fact. But in things wherein I stand in need of nothing but judgment, other men's reasons may serve to fortify my own, but have little power to dissuade me; I hear them all with civility and patience: but, to my recollection, I never made use of any but my own. With me, they are but flies and atoms, that confound and distract my will; I lay no great stress upon my opinions; but I lay as little upon those of others, and fortune rewards me accordingly: if I receive but little advice, I also give but little. I am seldom consulted, and still more seldom believed, and know no concern, either public or private, that has been mended or bettered by my advice. Even they whom fortune had in some sort tied to my direction, have more willingly suffered themselves to be governed by any other counsels than mine. And as a man who am as jealous of my repose as of my authority, I am better pleased that it should be so; in leaving me there, they humour what I profess, which is to settle and wholly contain myself within myself. I take a pleasure in being uninterested in other men's affairs, and disengaged from being their warranty, and responsible for what they do.

In all affairs that are past, be it how it will, I have very little regret; for this imagination puts me out of my pain, that they were so to fall out: they are in the great revolution of the world, and in the chain of stoical causes: your fancy cannot, by wish and imagination, move one tittle, but that the great current of things will not reverse both the past and the future.

As to the rest, I abominate that incidental repentance which old age brings along with it. He, who said of old,[12] that he was obliged to his age for having weaned him from pleasure, was of another opinion than I am; I can never think myself beholden to impotency, for any good it can do to me; "Nec tam aversa unquam videbitur ab opere suo providentia, ut

---

[11] Plutarch, Apothegm.

[12] Sophocles. Cicero, De Senect., c. 14.

debilitas inter optima inventa sit."[13] Our appetites are rare in old age; a profound satiety seizes us after the act; in this I see nothing of conscience; chagrin and weakness imprint in us a drowsy and rheumatic virtue. We must not suffer ourselves to be so wholly carried away by natural alterations, as to suffer our judgments to be imposed upon by them. Youth and pleasure have not formerly so far prevailed with me, that I did not well enough discern the face of vice in pleasure; neither does the distaste that years have brought me, so far prevail with me now, that I cannot discern pleasure in vice. Now that I am no more in my flourishing age, I judge as well of these things as if I were. I, who narrowly and strictly examine it, find my reason the very same it was in my most licentious age, except, perhaps, that 'tis weaker and more decayed by being grown older; and I find that the pleasure it refuses me upon the account of my bodily health, it would no more refuse now, in consideration of the health of my soul, than at any time heretofore. I do not repute it the more valiant for not being able to combat; my temptations are so broken and mortified, that they are not worth its opposition; holding but out my hands, I repel them. Should one present the old concupiscence before it, I fear it would have less power to resist it than heretofore; I do not discern that in itself it judges anything otherwise now, than it formerly did, nor that it has acquired any new light: wherefore, if there be convalescence, 'tis an enchanted one. Miserable kind of remedy, to owe one's health to one's disease! 'Tis not that our misfortune should perform this office, but the good fortune of our judgment. I am not to be made to do anything by persecutions and afflictions, but to curse them: that is for people who cannot be roused but by a whip. My reason is much more free in prosperity, and much more distracted, and put to't to digest pains than pleasures: I see best in a clear sky; health admonishes me more cheerfully, and to better purpose, than sickness. I did all that in me lay to reform and regulate myself from pleasures, at a time when I had health and vigour to enjoy them; I should be ashamed and envious, that the misery and misfortune of my old age should have credit over my good, healthful, sprightly, and vigorous years; and that men should estimate me, not by what I have been, but by what I have ceased to be.

In my opinion, 'tis the happy living, and not (as Antisthenes[14] said) the happy dying, in which human felicity consists. I have not made it my business to make a monstrous addition of a philosopher's tail to the head and body of a libertine; nor would I have this wretched remainder give the lie to the pleasant, sound, and long part of my life: I would present

---

[13] "Nor can Providence ever be seen so averse to her own work, that debility should be ranked amongst the best things." — Quintilian, Instit. Orat., v. 12.

[14] Diogenes Laertius, vi. 5.

myself uniformly throughout. Were I to live my life over again, I should
live it just as I have lived it; I neither complain of the past, nor do I fear
the future; and if I am not much deceived, I am the same within that I
am without. 'Tis one main obligation I have to my fortune, that the
succession of my bodily estate has been carried on according to the
natural seasons; I have seen the grass, the blossom, and the fruit; and
now see the withering; happily, however, because naturally. I bear the
infirmities I have the better, because they came not till I had reason to
expect them, and because also they make me with greater pleasure
remember that long felicity of my past life. My wisdom may have been
just the same in both ages; but it was more active, and of better grace
whilst young and sprightly, than now it is when broken, peevish, and
uneasy. I repudiate, then, these casual and painful reformations. God
must touch our hearts; our consciences must amend of themselves, by
the aid of our reason, and not by the decay of our appetites; pleasure is,
in itself, neither pale nor discoloured, to be discerned by dim and
decayed eyes.

We ought to love temperance for itself, and because God has
commanded that and chastity; but that which we are reduced to by
catarrhs, and for which I am indebted to the stone, is neither chastity
nor temperance; a man cannot boast that he despises and resists
pleasure, if he cannot see it, if he knows not what it is, and cannot
discern its graces, its force, and most alluring beauties; I know both the
one and the other, and may therefore the better say it. But, methinks,
our souls, in old age, are subject to more troublesome maladies and
imperfections than in youth; I said the same when young and when I
was reproached with the want of a beard; and I say so now that my grey
hairs give me some authority. We call the difficulty of our humours
and the disrelish of present things wisdom; but, in truth, we do not so
much forsake vices as we change them, and, in my opinion, for worse.
Besides a foolish and feeble pride, an impertinent prating, froward and
insociable humours, superstition, and a ridiculous desire of riches
when we have lost the use of them, I find there more envy, injustice,
and malice. Age imprints more wrinkles in the mind than it does on
the face; and souls are never, or very rarely seen, that in growing old do
not smell sour and musty. Man moves all together, both towards his
perfection and decay. In observing the wisdom of Socrates, and many
circumstances of his condemnation, I should dare to believe, that he
in some sort himself purposely, by collusion, contributed to it, seeing
that, at the age of seventy years, he might fear to suffer the lofty
motions of his mind to be cramped, and his wonted lustre obscured.
What strange metamorphoses do I see age every day make in many of
my acquaintance! 'Tis a potent malady, and that naturally and imper-
ceptibly steals into us; a vast provision of study and great precaution

are required to evade the imperfections it loads us with, or at least, to weaken their progress. I find that, notwithstanding all my entrenchments, it gets foot by foot upon me; I make the best resistance I can, but I do not know to what at last it will reduce me. But fall out what will, I am content the world may know, when I am fallen, from what I fell.

Of Three Commerces

WE MUST NOT rivet ourselves so fast to our humours and complexions: our chiefest sufficiency is to know how to apply ourselves to divers employments. 'Tis to be, but not to live, to keep a man's self tied and bound by necessity to one only course; those are the bravest souls that have in them the most variety and pliancy. Of this here is an honourable testimony of the elder Cato: "Huic versatile ingenium sic pariter ad omnia fuit, ut natum ad id unum diceres, quodcumque ageret."[1] Had I liberty to set myself forth after my own mode, there is no so graceful fashion to which I would be so fixed, as not to be able to disengage myself from it; life is an unequal, irregular, and multiform motion. 'Tis not to be a friend to one's self, much less a master — 'tis to be a slave, incessantly to be led by the nose by one's self, and to be so fixed in one's previous inclinations, that one cannot turn aside, nor writhe one's neck out of the collar. I say this now in this part of my life, wherein I find I cannot easily disengage myself from the importunity of my soul, which cannot ordinarily amuse itself but in things of limited range, nor employ itself otherwise than entirely and with all its force; upon the lightest subject offered it swells and stretches it to that degree as therein to employ its utmost power; wherefore, its idleness is to me a very painful labour, and very prejudicial to my health. Most men's minds require foreign matter to exercise and enliven them; mine has rather need of it to sit still and repose itself, "Vitia otii negotio discutienda sunt,"[2] for its chiefest and hardest study is to study itself. Books are to it a sort of employment that debauch it from its study. Upon the first thoughts that possess it, it begins to bustle and make trial of its vigour in all directions, exercises its power of handling, now making trial of force, now fortifying, moderating, and ranging itself by the way of grace and order. It has of its own wherewith to rouse its faculties: nature has given to it, as to all

---

[1] "His parts were so pliable to all uses, that a man would think he had been born only for precisely that which he was at any time doing." — Livy, xxxix. 49.

[2] "The vices of sloth are to be shaken off by business." — Seneca, Ep. 56.

others, matter enough of its own to make advantage of, and subjects proper enough where it may either invent or judge.

Meditation is a powerful and full study to such as can effectually taste and employ themselves; I had rather fashion my soul than furnish it. There is no employment, either more weak or more strong, than that of entertaining a man's own thoughts, according as the soul is; the greatest men make it their whole business, "quibus vivere est cogitare;"[3] nature has therefore favoured it with this privilege, that there is nothing we can do so long, nor any action to which we more frequently and with greater facility addict ourselves. 'Tis the business of the gods, says Aristotle,[4] and from which both their beatitude and ours proceed.

The principal use of reading to me is, that by various objects it rouses my reason, and employs my judgment, not my memory. Few conversations detain me without force and effort; it is true that beauty and elegance of speech take as much or more with me than the weight and depth of the subject; and forasmuch as I am apt to be sleepy in all other communication, and give but the rind of my attention, it often falls out that in such poor and pitiful discourses, mere chatter, I either make drowsy, unmeaning answers, unbecoming a child, and ridiculous, or more foolishly and rudely still, maintain an obstinate silence. I have a pensive way that withdraws me into myself, and, with that, a heavy and childish ignorance of many very ordinary things, by which two qualities I have earned this, that men may truly relate five or six as ridiculous tales of me as of any other man whatever.

But, to proceed in my subject, this difficult complexion of mine renders me very nice in my conversation with men, whom I must cull and pick out for my purpose; and unfits me for common society. We live and negotiate with the people; if their conversation be troublesome to us, if we disdain to apply ourselves to mean and vulgar souls (and the mean and vulgar are often as regular as those of the finest thread, and all wisdom is folly that does not accommodate itself to the common ignorance), we must no more intermeddle either with other men's affairs or our own; for business, both public and private, has to do with these people. The least forced and most natural motions of the soul are the most beautiful; the best employments, those that are least strained. Good God! how good an office does wisdom to those whose desires it limits to their power! that is the most useful knowledge: "what a man can," was ever the sentence Socrates was so much in love with. A motto of great substance.

We must moderate and adapt our desires to the nearest and easiest to be acquired things. Is it not a foolish humour of mine to separate myself

---

[3] "To whom to live is to think." — Cicero, Tusc. Quæs., v. 28.

[4] Moral. ad Nicom., x. 8.

from a thousand to whom my fortune has conjoined me, and without whom I cannot live, and cleave to one or two who are out of my intercourse; or, rather a fantastic desire of a thing I cannot obtain? My gentle and easy manners, enemies of all sourness and harshness, may easily enough have secured me from envy and animosities; to be beloved, I do not say, but never any man gave less occasion of being hated; but the coldness of my conversation has, reasonably enough, deprived me of the goodwill of many, who are to be excused if they interpret it in another and worse sense.

I am very capable of contracting and maintaining rare and exquisite friendships; for, by reason that I so greedily seize upon such acquaintance as fit my liking, I throw myself with such violence upon them that I hardly fail to stick, and to make an impression where I hit; as I have often made happy proof. In ordinary friendships I am somewhat cold and shy, for my motion is not natural, if not with full sail; besides which, my fortune having in my youth given me a relish for one sole and perfect friendship has, in truth, created in me a kind of distaste to others, and too much imprinted in my fancy that it is a beast of company, as the ancient said, but not of the herd.[5] And also I have a natural difficulty of communicating myself by halves, with the modifications and the servile and jealous prudence required in the conversation of numerous and imperfect friendships: and we are principally enjoined to these in this age of ours, when we cannot talk of the world but either with danger or falsehood.

Yet do I very well discern, that he who has the conveniences (I mean the essential conveniences) of life for his end, as I have, ought to fly these difficulties and delicacy of humour, as much as the plague. I should commend a soul of several stages, that knows both how to stretch and to slacken itself; that finds itself at ease in all conditions whither fortune leads it; that can discourse with a neighbour, of his building, his hunting, his quarrels; that can chat with a carpenter or a gardener with pleasure. I envy those who can render themselves familiar with the meanest of their followers, and talk with them in their own way; and dislike the advice of Plato,[6] that men should always speak in a magisterial tone to their servants, whether men or women, without being sometimes facetious and familiar; for besides the reasons I have given, 'tis inhuman and unjust, to set so great a value upon this pitiful prerogative of fortune; and the polities, wherein less disparity is permitted betwixt masters and servants, seem to me the most equitable. Others study how to raise and elevate their minds; I, how to humble mine, and to bring it low; 'tis only vicious in extension.

---

[5] Plutarch, On the Plurality of Friends, c. 2.

[6] Laws, vi.

"Narras et genus Æaci,
Et pugnata sacro bella sub Ilio;
Quo Chium pretio cadum
Mercemur, quis aquam temperet ignibus,
Quo præbente domum, et quota,
Pelignis caream frigoribus, taces."[7]

Thus, as the Lacedæmonian valour stood in need of moderation, and of the sweet and harmonious sound of flutes to soften it in battle, lest they should precipitate themselves into temerity and fury, whereas all other nations commonly make use of harsh and shrill sounds, and of loud and imperious cries, to incite and heat the soldier's courage to the last degree: so, methinks, contrary to the usual method, in the practice of our minds, we have for the most part more need of lead than of wings; of temperance and composedness than of ardour and agitation. But, above all things, 'tis in my opinion egregiously to play the fool, to put on the grave airs of a man of lofty mind amongst those who are nothing of the sort: ever to speak in print, "favellár in punta di forchetta."[8] You must let yourself down to those with whom you converse; and sometimes affect ignorance: lay aside power and subtilty in common conversation; to preserve decorum and order 'tis enough—nay, crawl on the earth, if they so desire it.

The learned often stumble at this stone; they will always be parading their pedantic science, and strew their books everywhere; they have, in these days, so filled the cabinets and ears of the ladies with them, that if they have lost the substance, they at least retain the words; so as in all discourse upon all sorts of subjects, how mean and common soever, they speak and write after a new and learned way;

"Hoc sermone pavent, hoc iram, gaudia, curas,
Hoc cuncta effundunt animi secreta; quid ultra?
Concumbunt docte;"[9]

and quote Plato and Aquinas, in things the first man they meet could determine as well; the learning that cannot penetrate their souls, hangs still upon the tongue. If people of quality will be persuaded by me, they shall content themselves with setting out their proper and natural treasures; they conceal and cover their beauties under others that are none

---

[7] "You tell us long stories about the race of Æacus, and the battles fought at sacred Ilium; but what to give for a cask of Chian wine, who shall prepare the warm bath, and in whose house, and when we shall flee the Pelignian cold, you do not tell us."—Horace, Od. iii. 19, 3.

[8] "To talk with the point of a fork."

[9] "In this same learned language do they express their fears, their anger, their joys, their cares; in this pour out all their secrets; what more? they lie with their lovers learnedly."—Juvenal, vi. 189.

of theirs: 'tis a great folly to put out their own light and shine by a borrowed lustre: they are interred and buried under art, "de capsula totæ."[10] It is because they do not sufficiently know themselves, or do themselves justice: the world has nothing fairer than they; 'tis for them to honour the arts, and to paint painting. What need have they of anything, but to live beloved and honoured? They have, and know, but too much for this: they need do no more but rouse and heat a little the faculties they have of their own. When I see them tampering with rhetoric, law, logic, and other drugs, so improper and unnecessary for their business, I begin to suspect that the men who inspire them with such fancies, do it that they may govern them upon that account; for what other excuse can I contrive? It is enough that they can, without our instruction, compose the graces of their eyes to gaiety, severity, sweetness, and season a denial with asperity, suspense, or favour: they need not another to interpret what we speak for their service; with this knowledge, they command with a switch, and rule both the tutors and the schools. But if, nevertheless, it angers them to give place to us in anything whatever, and will, out of curiosity, have their share in books, poetry is a diversion proper for them; 'tis a wanton, subtle, dissembling and prating art, all pleasure and all show, like themselves. They may also extract several commodities from history. In philosophy, out of the moral part of it, they may select such instructions as will teach them to judge of our humours and conditions, to defend themselves from our treacheries, to regulate the ardour of their own desires, to manage their liberty, to lengthen the pleasures of life, and gently to bear the inconstancy of a lover, the rudeness of a husband, and the importunity of years, wrinkles, and the like. This is the utmost of what I would allow them in the sciences.

There are some particular natures that are private and retired: my natural way is proper for communication, and apt to lay me open; I am all without and in sight, born for society and friendship. The solitude that I love myself and recommend to others, is chiefly no other than to withdraw my thoughts and affections into myself; to restrain and check, not my steps, but my own cares and desires, resigning all foreign solicitude, and mortally avoiding servitude and obligation, and not so much the crowd of men, as the crowd of business. Local solitude, to say the truth, rather gives me more room, and sets me more at large; I more readily throw myself upon affairs of state and the world, when I am alone; at the Louvre, and in the bustle of the court, I fold myself within my own skin; the crowd thrusts me upon myself; and I never entertain myself so wantonly, with so much licence, or so especially, as in places of respect and ceremonious prudence: our follies do not make me laugh,

---

[10] "Painted and perfumed from head to foot." — Seneca, Ep. 115.

but our wisdom does. I am naturally no enemy to a court life; I have therein passed a good part of my own, and am of a humour cheerfully to frequent great company, provided it be by intervals and at my own time: but this softness of judgment whereof I speak, ties me perforce to solitude. Even at home, amidst a numerous family, and in a house sufficiently frequented, I see people enough, but rarely such with whom I delight to converse; and I there reserve both for myself and others an unusual liberty: there is in my house no such thing as ceremony, ushering, or waiting upon people down to the coach, and such other troublesome ceremonies as our courtesy enjoins (O servile and importunate custom!) Every one there governs himself according to his own method; let who will speak his thoughts, I sit mute, meditating and shut up in my closet, without any offence to my guests.

The men, whose society and familiarity I covet, are those they call sincere and able men; and the image of these makes me disrelish the rest. It is, if rightly taken, the rarest of our forms, and a form that we chiefly owe to nature. The end of this commerce is simply privacy, frequentation and conference, the exercise of souls, without other fruit. In our discourse, all subjects are alike to me; let there be neither weight, nor depth, 'tis all one: there is yet grace and pertinency; all there is tinted with a mature and constant judgment, and mixed with goodness, freedom, gaiety, and friendship. 'Tis not only in talking of the affairs of kings and state, that our wits discover their force and beauty, but every whit as much in private conferences. I understand my men even by their silence and smiles; and better discover them, perhaps, at table, than in the council. Hippomachus said[11] very well, "that he could know the good wrestlers by only seeing them walk in the street." If learning please to step into our talk, it shall not be rejected, not magisterial, imperious, and importunate, as it commonly is, but suffragan and docile itself; we there only seek to pass away our time; when we have a mind to be instructed and preached to, we will go seek this in its throne; please let it humble itself to us for the nonce; for, useful and profitable as it is, I imagine that, at need, we may manage well enough without it, and do our business without its assistance. A well-descended soul, and practised in the conversation of men, will of herself render herself sufficiently agreeable; art is nothing but the counterpart and register of what such souls produce.

The conversation also of beautiful and well-bred women is for me a sweet commerce: "nam nos quoque oculos eruditos habemus."[12] If the soul has not therein so much to enjoy, as in the first, the bodily senses, which participate more of this, bring it to a proportion near to, though,

---

[11] Plutarch, Life of Dion., c. 1.

[12] "For we also have eyes that are versed in the matter." — Cicero, Paradox, v. 2.

in my opinion, not equal to the other. But 'tis a commerce wherein a man must stand a little upon his guard, especially those of a warm temperament, such as mine. I there scalded myself in my youth, and suffered all the torments that poets say are to befall those who precipitate themselves into love without order and judgment: it is true, that the whipping has made me wiser since:

"Quicumque Argolica de classe Capharea fugit,
   Semper ab Euboicis vela retorquet aquis."[13]

'Tis folly to fix all a man's thoughts upon it, and to engage in it with a furious and indiscreet affection; but, on the other hand, to engage there without love and without inclination, like comedians, to play a common part, without putting anything to it of his own but words, is indeed to provide for his safety, but, withal, after as cowardly a manner as he who should abandon his honour, profit, or pleasure, for fear of ordinary danger; for it is certain that from such a practice, they who set it on foot can expect no fruit that can please or satisfy a noble soul. A man must have, in good earnest, desired that which he, in good earnest, expects to have a pleasure in enjoying; I say, though fortune should unjustly favour their dissimulation; which often falls out, because there is none of the sex, let her be as ugly as the devil, who does not think herself well worthy to be beloved, and who does not prefer herself before other women, either for her youth, the colour of her hair, or her graceful motion (for there are no more women universally and throughout ugly, than there are women universally and throughout beautiful, and such of the Brahmin virgins as have no other beauty to recommend them, the people being assembled by the common crier to that effect, come out into the market-place to expose their matrimonial parts to public view, to try if these at least are not of temptation sufficient to get them husbands); consequently, there is not one who does not easily suffer herself to be overcome by the first vow that is made to serve her. Now from this common and ordinary treachery of the men of the present day, that must fall out which we already experimentally see, either that they rally together, and separate themselves by themselves to evade us, or else form their discipline by the example we give them, play their parts of the farce as we do ours, and give themselves up to the sport, without passion, care, or love: "Neque affectui suo, aut alieno, obnoxiæ:"[14] believing, according to the persuasion of Lysias in Plato,[15] that they may with more

---

[13] "Whoever of the Grecian fleet has escaped the Capharean rocks, ever takes care to steer from those of the Eubœan sea." — Ovid, Trist., i. 1, 83.

[14] "Incapable of attachment, insensible to that of others." — Tacitus, Annal., xiii. 45.

[15] In Phæd.

utility and convenience surrender themselves up to us the less we love them; where it will fall out, as in comedies, that the people will have as much pleasure or more than the comedians. For my part, I no more acknowledge a Venus without a Cupid, than a mother without issue: they are things that mutually lend and owe their essence to one another. Thus this cheat recoils upon him who is guilty of it; it does not cost him much, indeed, but he also gets little or nothing by it. They who have made Venus a goddess have taken notice that her principal beauty was incorporeal and spiritual: but the Venus whom these people hunt after is not so much as human, nor indeed brutal; the very beasts will not accept it so gross and so earthly; we see that imagination and desire often heat and incite them before the body does; we see in both the one sex and the other, they have in the herd choice and particular election in their affections, and that they have amongst themselves a long commerce of good will. Even those to whom old age denies the practice of their desire, still tremble, neigh, and twitter for love; we see them, before the act, full of hope and ardour, and when the body has played its game, yet please themselves with the sweet remembrance of the past delight; some that swell with pride after they have performed, and others who, tired and sated, still by vociferation express a triumphing joy. He who has nothing to do but only to discharge his body of a natural necessity, need not trouble others with so curious preparations: it is not meat for a gross, coarse appetite.

As one who does not desire that men should think me better than I am, I will here say this as to the errors of my youth. Not only from the danger of impairing my health (and yet I could not be so careful but that I had two light mischances), but moreover upon the account of contempt, I have seldom given myself up to common and mercenary embraces: I would heighten the pleasure by the difficulty, by desire, and a certain kind of glory: and was of Tiberius's mind, who[16] in his amours was as much taken with modesty and birth as any other quality; and of the courtesan Flora's humour,[17] who never prostituted herself to less than a dictator, a consul, or a censor, and took pleasure in the dignity of her lovers. Doubtless pearls and gold tissue, titles and train, add something to it.

As to the rest, I had a great esteem for wit, provided the person was not exceptionable; for, to confess the truth, if the one or the other of these two attractions must of necessity be wanting, I should rather have quitted that of the understanding, that has its use in better things; but in the subject of love, a subject principally relating to the senses of seeing and touching, something may be done without the graces of the mind:

---

[16] Tacitus, Annal., vi. 1.

[17] Bayle, art. Flora; Brantome, Des Femmes Galantes.

without the graces of the body, nothing. Beauty is the true prerogative of women, and so peculiarly their own, that ours, though naturally requiring another sort of feature, is never in its lustre but when youthful and beardless, a sort of confused image of theirs. 'Tis said, that such as serve the Grand Signior upon the account of beauty, who are an infinite number, are, at the latest, dismissed at two and twenty years of age. Reason, prudence, and the offices of friendship are better found amongst men, and therefore it is, that they govern the affairs of the world.

These two commerces are fortuitous, and depending upon others; the one is troublesome by its rarity, the other withers with age, so that they could never have been sufficient for the business of my life. That of books, which is the third, is much more certain, and much more our own. It yields all other advantages to the two first; but has the constancy and facility of its service for its own share. It goes side by side with me in my whole course, and everywhere is assisting me: it comforts me in my old age and solitude; it eases me of a troublesome weight of idleness, and delivers me at all hours from company that I dislike: it blunts the point of griefs, if they are not extreme, and have not got an entire possession of my soul. To divert myself from a troublesome fancy, 'tis but to run to my books; they presently fix me to them and drive the other out of my thoughts; and do not mutiny at seeing that I have only recourse to them for want of other more real, natural, and lively commodities; they always receive me with the same kindness. He may well go a foot, they say, who leads his horse in his hand; and our James, king of Naples and Sicily, who, handsome, young and healthful, caused himself to be carried about on a barrow, extended upon a pitiful mattress in a poor robe of grey cloth, and a cap of the same, but attended withal by a royal train of litters, led horses of all sorts, gentlemen and officers, did yet herein represent a tender and unsteady authority: "The sick man is not to be pitied, who has his cure in his sleeve." In the experience and practice of this maxim, which is a very true one, consists all the benefit I reap from books; and yet I make as little use of them, almost, as those who know them not: I enjoy them as a miser does his money, in knowing that I may enjoy them when I please: my mind is satisfied with this right of possession. I never travel without books, either in peace or war; and yet sometimes I pass over several days, and sometimes months, without looking on them: I will read by-and-by, say I to myself, or to-morrow, or when I please; and in the interim, time steals away without any inconvenience. For it is not to be imagined to what degree I please myself and rest content in this consideration, that I have them by me to divert myself with them when I am so disposed, and to call to mind what a refreshment they are to my life. 'Tis the best viaticum I have yet found out for this human journey, and I very much pity those men of understanding who are unprovided of it. I the rather accept of any other sort of diversion, how light soever, because this can never fail me.

When at home, I a little more frequent my library, whence I overlook at once all the concerns of my family. 'Tis situated at the entrance into my house, and I thence see under me my garden, court, and base-court, and almost all parts of the building. There I turn over now one book, and then another, on various subjects without method or design. One while I meditate, another I record and dictate, as I walk to and fro, such whimsies as these I present to you here. 'Tis in the third storey of a tower, of which the ground room is my chapel, the second storey a chamber with a withdrawing-room and closet, where I often lie, to be more retired; and above is a great wardrobe. This formerly was the most useless part of the house. I there pass away both most of the days of my life and most of the hours of those days. In the night I am never there. There is by the side of it a cabinet handsome enough, with a fireplace very commodiously contrived, and plenty of light: and were I not more afraid of the trouble than the expense — the trouble that frights me from all business, I could very easily adjoin on either side, and on the same floor, a gallery of an hundred paces long, and twelve broad, having found walls already raised for some other design, to the requisite height. Every place of retirement requires a walk: my thoughts sleep if I sit still; my fancy does not go by itself, as when my legs move it: and all those who study without a book are in the same condition. The figure of my study is round, and there is no more open wall than what is taken up by my table and my chair, so that the remaining parts of the circle present me a view of all my books at once, ranged upon five rows of shelves round about me. It has three noble and free prospects, and is sixteen paces in diameter. I am not so continually there in winter; for my house is built upon an eminence, as its name imports, and no part of it is so much exposed to the wind and weather as this, which pleases me the better, as being of more difficult access and a little remote, as well upon the account of exercise, as also being there more retired from the crowd. 'Tis there that I am in my kingdom, and there I endeavour to make myself an absolute monarch, and to sequester this one corner from all society, conjugal, filial, and civil; elsewhere I have but verbal authority only, and of a confused essence. That man, in my opinion, is very miserable, who has not at home where to be by himself, where to entertain himself alone, or to conceal himself from others. Ambition sufficiently plagues her proselytes, by keeping them always in show, like the statue of a public square: "Magna servitus est magna fortuna."[18] They cannot so much as be private in the water-closet. I have thought nothing so severe in the austerity of life that our monks affect, as what I

---

[18] "A great fortune is a great slavery." — Seneca, De Consol. ad Polyb., c. 26.

have observed in some of their communities; namely, by rule to have a perpetual society of place, and numerous persons present in every action whatever; and think it much more supportable to be always alone, than never to be so.

If any one shall tell me that it is to undervalue the muses, to make use of them only for sport and to pass away the time, I shall tell him, that he does not know, so well as I, the value of the sport, the pleasure, and the pastime; I can hardly forbear to add that all other end is ridiculous. I live from hand to mouth, and, with reverence be it spoken, I only live for myself; there all my designs terminate. I studied, when young, for ostentation; since, to make myself a little wiser; and now for my diversion, but never for any profit. A vain and prodigal humour I had after this sort of furniture, not only for the supplying my own need, but, moreover, for ornament and outward show, I have since quite cured myself of.

Books have many charming qualities to such as know how to choose them; but every good has its ill; 'tis a pleasure that is not pure and clean, no more than others: it has its inconveniences, and great ones too. The soul indeed is exercised therein; but the body, the care of which I must withal never neglect, remains in the meantime without action, and grows heavy and sombre. I know no excess more prejudicial to me, nor more to be avoided in this my declining age.

These have been my three favourite and particular occupations; I speak not of those I owe to the world by civil obligation.

DOVER · THRIFT · EDITIONS

All books complete and unabridged. All 5³⁄₁₆" × 8¹⁄₄", paperbound.
Just $1.00–$2.00 in U.S.A.

A selection of the more than 100 titles in the series:

FLATLAND: A ROMANCE OF MANY DIMENSIONS, Edwin A. Abbott. 96pp. 27263-X $1.00

DOVER BEACH AND OTHER POEMS, Matthew Arnold. 112pp. 28037-3 $1.00

CIVIL WAR STORIES, Ambrose Bierce. 128pp. 28038-1 $1.00

THE DEVIL'S DICTIONARY, Ambrose Bierce. 144pp. 27542-6 $1.00

SONGS OF INNOCENCE AND SONGS OF EXPERIENCE, William Blake. 64pp. 27051-3 $1.00

SONNETS FROM THE PORTUGUESE AND OTHER POEMS, Elizabeth Barrett Browning. 64pp. 27052-1 $1.00

MY LAST DUCHESS AND OTHER POEMS, Robert Browning. 128pp. 27783-6 $1.00

SELECTED POEMS, George Gordon, Lord Byron. 112pp. 27784-4 $1.00

ALICE'S ADVENTURES IN WONDERLAND, Lewis Carroll. 96pp. 27543-4 $1.00

O PIONEERS!, Willa Cather. 128pp. 27785-2 $1.00

THE CHERRY ORCHARD, Anton Chekhov. 64pp. 26682-6 $1.00

THE AWAKENING, Kate Chopin. 128pp. 27786-0 $1.00

THE RIME OF THE ANCIENT MARINER AND OTHER POEMS, Samuel Taylor Coleridge. 80pp. 27266-4 $1.00

HEART OF DARKNESS, Joseph Conrad. 80pp. 26464-5 $1.00

THE RED BADGE OF COURAGE, Stephen Crane. 112pp. 26465-3 $1.00

A CHRISTMAS CAROL, Charles Dickens. 80pp. 26865-9 $1.00

THE CRICKET ON THE HEARTH AND OTHER CHRISTMAS STORIES, Charles Dickens. 128pp. 28039-X $1.00

SELECTED POEMS, Emily Dickinson. 64pp. 26466-1 $1.00

SELECTED POEMS, John Donne. 96pp. 27788-7 $1.00

NOTES FROM THE UNDERGROUND, Fyodor Dostoyevsky. 96pp. 27053-X $1.00

SIX GREAT SHERLOCK HOLMES STORIES, Sir Arthur Conan Doyle. 112pp. 27055-6 $1.00

THE SOULS OF BLACK FOLK, W. E. B. Du Bois. 176pp. 28041-1 $2.00

MEDEA, Euripides. 64pp. 27548-5 $1.00

A BOY'S WILL AND NORTH OF BOSTON, Robert Frost. 112pp. (Available in U.S. only) 26866-7 $1.00

WHERE ANGELS FEAR TO TREAD, E. M. Forster. 128pp. (Available in U.S. only) 27791-7 $1.00

FAUST, PART ONE, Johann Wolfgang von Goethe. 192pp. 28046-2 $2.00

THE SCARLET LETTER, Nathaniel Hawthorne. 192pp. 28048-9 $2.00

A DOLL'S HOUSE, Henrik Ibsen. 80pp. 27062-9 $1.00

THE TURN OF THE SCREW, Henry James. 96pp. 26684-2 $1.00

VOLPONE, Ben Jonson. 112pp. 28049-7 $1.00

DUBLINERS, James Joyce. 160pp. 26870-5 $1.00

A PORTRAIT OF THE ARTIST AS A YOUNG MAN, James Joyce. 192pp. 28050-0 $2.00

LYRIC POEMS, John Keats. 80pp. 26871-3 $1.00

THE BOOK OF PSALMS, King James Bible. 144pp. 27541-8 $1.00